Stefan Bucza

Best Climbers

HAMLYN

Publishing Director Laura Bamford
Creative Director Keith Martin
Executive Editor Julian Brown
Design Manager Bryan Dunn
Editor Karen O'Grady
Designer Michael Whitehead and TT Design
Production Karina Han
Picture Research Jenny Faithfull

First published in Great Britain in 1994
by Hamlyn
an imprint of Octopus Publishing Group Ltd
Michelin House, 81 Fulham Road, London SW3 6RB

This edition published in 1998

Produced by Toppan
Printed in China

ISBN 0 600 59737 7

A catalogue of this book is available at the
British Library

CONTENTS

INTRODUCTION

I still see far too many gardens that are merely two-dimensional creations. They have beds and borders, quite possibly of very great beauty and sometimes of rather intricate and ingenious complexity. But their owners haven't realized the full potential of their site because they have forgotten to explore upwards. It is upwards, the third gardening dimension, that is the realm of climbing plants and it is no exaggeration to say that you can, if not exactly double the size of your garden, at least increase your growing area by a surprising percentage through the use of climbers.

Climbers and shrubs can be grown to hide fences and other unsightly objects

There is nothing intrinsically unique about a climbing plant and in fact the boundary between climbers and non-climbers is much more blurred than many people imagine. To put it simply, a climber is no more than a plant that cannot support itself; it requires something on which to lean or to cling to. In their natural habitat, the support is very often provided by other plants, most notably trees or large shrubs, but cliffs and rock faces are also utilized by some species while others merely produce a tangle on the ground that become larger as the plant piles upwards upon itself.

The adoption of a climbing habit is no reflection of the relative woodiness of the stems for there are plenty of very woody, perennial climbers, such as vines and clematis, that have pliable stems, just as there are of non-woody annuals such as *Tropaeolum*. And there are also numerous examples of border-line plants, like the exquisite white jasmine *Jasminum officinale,* which can just about survive as a free-standing shrub but is much better when grown up some form of prop.

In this book I have described a wide selection of plants that fulfil my criteria as climbers and have deliberately included several that will be unfamiliar but which are worthy of wider recognition. The only major group of climbers not covered here are roses which are dealt with in detail in *Best Roses*. I have also excluded those shrubs (often called wall shrubs) such as pyracanthas that are usually trained against walls but which can perfectly well be free-standing. Despite these restrictions, my problem has been what climbers to omit.

There are two main reasons for planting a climber, reasons that may well overlap. The plant may be needed to do a particular job, by which I mean covering an unsightly object or providing a screen to give shelter or privacy, or it may simply be wanted for its ornamental appeal. But whatever the reason for purchase, you will want to choose the right plant the first time and to achieve this it's helpful to consider a check list of characteristics.

Tropaeolum **twines around a support**

SELF-CLINGING

Ivy is the best example of a self-clinging plant. It can attach itself to a vertical surface, without needing to be tied in or pegged, by means of adhesive pads at the ends of tiny aerial roots. Even a surface as smooth as a painted window frame is no bar to a plant such as ivy, and because it clings so tightly, paintwork and even old bricks and stone can be damaged – at least when you try to pull the thing off its support. Not many garden climbers are self-clinging and apart from the ivies the most important are the *Parthenocissus* vines, including Virginia creeper and Boston ivy, both of which are ideal for covering large walls or chimney stacks, far out of reach of gardeners with tying wire. The adhesive pads of *Parthenocissus*, however, are borne not at the tips of aerial roots but on tendrils (see below).

NON-SELF-CLINGING

The non-self-clinging species can be roughly divided into twiners, tendril-climbers and grapplers. Twiners grasp their supports by wrapping their entire stems around them, and include such widely differing plants as wisterias and runner beans. Very commonly, they embrace other stems on the same plant, a group of stems thus becoming intertwined rather like a rope. There seems to be no logic or reason why some species twine clockwise and others anti-clockwise; but contrary to what is often asked, no, they don't change direction in the southern hemisphere.

Tendrils are short, string-like lengths of grasping organ. Sometimes, as with clematis, these are modified leaf stalks; in other instances, as with grapevines, they appear to be modified stems: but some plants possess both and in a number of cases it is impossible to decide what the original nature of the tendril might have been. In many species, moreover, the tendrils are branched to give greater grasping efficiency, while in *Parthenocissus* and related plants, as I have mentioned, the tendrils themselves are further modified to become self-clinging.

Plants that grapple have an apparently much cruder system, based on spines, generally backward pointing. Spines, too, may have different origins; those most commonly found on climbers such as roses are modified extensions of the stem, whereas others, like those of gorse and cacti (not of course climbing plants), are modified leaves.

Self-clinging *Hedera colchica* 'Gloire de Marengo' growing up a wall

HARDINESS

The plant must be sufficiently hardy to survive all year round in your garden. Here, climbers are generally at an advantage over other types of plant because a wall, fence or other support will provide some shelter from the wind and will often radiate warmth. So a climber may survive while an equally hardy or tender plant may fail in the open garden. The minimum winter temperature that the plant can tolerate is the most important measure and I have indicated this for each of the plants in the book. It's also worth bearing in mind, however, that a plant that produces its flowers or new leaves early in the spring may suffer from late frosts, so if these happen to be common in your area you may find that growth is checked in some seasons.

WIND TOLERANCE

Many plants that can survive very low temperatures in calm weather may, nonetheless, be damaged by cold winter winds, and also by winds that are laden with salt. Salty winds will obviously be important at the coast but salt can also be thrown up at roadsides in winter and it is then that many evergreen climbers suffer from leaf scorch and browning; they therefore don't make good subjects for planting very close to roads.

NEED FOR SUN

Many climbers, especially flowering types, will only perform satisfactorily in a sunny position but may tolerate light shade. Others may be tolerant of fairly intense shade and a few actually yield their most intense flower colour away from the sun's glare. It is essential to check the relative sunniness and aspect of your chosen spot before planting a climber with specific needs.

EVERGREEN OR DECIDUOUS?

An evergreen plant will clearly give year-round cover whereas a deciduous one will not. But the choice may not be quite that simple. As I've already indicated, evergreens can be damaged by salt or cold in winter and they will also offer more of a barrier to the wind. In winter, therefore, when the winds are likely to be strong, a climber on a free-standing structure such as a pergola may create a stability problem and even cause the structure itself to be damaged. Evergreens may similarly cause stability problems in winter if they are used to clothe trellis atop a fence or wall. And of course, continuous foliage cover may not be the most important factor. Rather few hardy evergreen climbers have attractive flowers while, conversely, the foliage of many deciduous climbers offers the spectacle of splendid autumn colours before it drops.

FLOWERS

While an evergreen or at least a predominantly foliage climber is generally the best way to cover a large surface or object, a flowering plant, such as *Lathyrus latifolius* (see right, above), will win almost every time for small-scale ornamental effect. But the length of the flowering period varies enormously – wisterias, for instance, have their optimum effect for about ten days in spring whereas some types of hybrid clematis such as 'The President' will be more or less continuously in bloom right through the summer. Think carefully about the amount and type of colour elsewhere in your garden too; do you really want the blue climber on your house wall to be in flower at the same time as the orange roses in the bed in front of it? And do give some thought to fragrance which varies considerably even among varieties of the same species – within the very popular spring-flowering *Clematis montana* for instance, there are types such as 'Elizabeth' with a delicate perfume and others, like the larger flowered 'Tetrarose' with very little.

Lathyrus latifolius **'White Pearl'**

Fallopia baldschuanica **engulfing a tree**

It is because climbers are so often planted in relatively impoverished and dry conditions close to a wall or other support, that they respond particularly well to supplementary feeding and watering. In fact, the improvement after feeding is sometimes so great that gardeners scarcely recognize their own plants. But what fertilizer to use and with what frequency varies from plant to plant and I have indicated this in the individual accounts. By and large, however, a young perennial climber should be fed twice, once as growth starts in the spring and once again around mid-summer.

Greedy feeding Thunbergia alata

FOLIAGE CLIMBERS

For foliage climbers, the most useful fertilizer will be a balanced general purpose blend such as the organically based fish, blood and bone with an approximate N:P:K ratio of 5:5:6, or a comparable artificial mixture with a ratio of 7:7:7, such as Growmore. I generally find the artificials to be too fast acting for optimum results and their benefits don't last very long. It's worth a reminder that proprietary fish, blood and bone with the above composition is only organically *based*, not entirely organic as many organic gardeners seem to believe. This is because a mixture comprising only fish meal, dried blood and bone meal would be deficient in potash, so potassium sulphate is added to produce a more useful blend. Balanced fertilizers such as these should be applied at a rate of around 70g per sq m (2oz per sq yd) which in practice means a small handful scattered around each plant.

FLOWERING CLIMBERS

For flowering climbers, you can make do with a general fertilizer but better results are usually obtained with one that contains proportionally more potash to encourage flowering. I use proprietary rose fertilizer of which there are now organic and artificial types; these should also be applied at approximately 70g per sq m (2oz per sq yd). But there's not much point in dumping dry fertilizer powder around a climber growing in inherently dry soil, for it will remain on the surface, become caked and be of no benefit to the plant. Ideally, it should be applied after rain, raked into the soil surface and then watered in with a watering can or hose.

PERENNIAL CLIMBERS

In order to try to maintain the soil around perennial climbers in a moist condition, a mulch should be applied in spring and again in autumn. But do remember that the soil must be wet initially – a mulch will keep a dry soil dry just as much as it will a wet one wet. By and large, the most useful mulching material is home-produced garden compost or leaf mould but some plants will fare better with well-rotted manure (I have indicated where this is so in the individual descriptions) and a few, acid-loving types benefit from a mulch of chopped conifer needles.

HERBACEOUS CLIMBERS AND MOST ANNUALS

All herbaceous climbers such as the golden hop and almost all annual climbers raised from seed such as morning glory need feeding rather differently. A small amount of general fertilizer should be raked into the soil around the plants in spring, but they also require regular feeds every one or two weeks with a liquid mixture which is high in potash, such as a proprietary tomato fertilizer. At least part of this liquid feed may be applied through the foliage with a sprayer for the quickest results. Fast growing woody perennial climbers such as *Clematis* will benefit from additional feeding in this way too. Finally, of course, annual climbers, being generally more shallow rooted, need to be watered more regularly and particularly carefully.

A notable exception to the need for feeding annual climbers lies with the climbing nasturtiums (*Tropaeolum*) which should be grown in poor soil and starved of food in order to encourage flower production at the expense of leaves.

SOIL

I'm sure that climbers have a harder time than most other types of garden plant because the soil close to their support is likely to be impoverished in some way. If they are planted against a wall or fence, the soil will be dry as it is sheltered from rain to a considerable degree. And if the support is provided by a hedge or a tree, the situation will be compounded by a shortage of nutrients. Once the climber is established, of course, regular feeding and watering will help maintain it in a healthy state but initial preparation before planting is vitally important if your plant really is to produce of its best.

All soils contain greater or lesser amounts of sand, silt, clay and humus, their relative proportions giving each soil type its characteristic features.

CLAY SOIL

A soil with a high clay content will be slow to warm up in spring but then retains warmth well and is likely to be generously supplied with nutrients. In dry conditions, however, such as those in which climbers often find themselves, it can be hard and impenetrable whereas in wet winter weather, it may become waterlogged.

SANDY SOIL

Unlike a clay soil, a light sandy soil will warm up quickly, cool down quickly and, being free-draining, will lose both water and nutrients rapidly.

HUMUS

Humus (part-decomposed organic matter) will improve both types of soil for it contains natural gel-like substances that bind together soil particles to form crumbs and also help the retention of moisture by their sponge-like properties. It is important always to dig in plenty of compost, manure or other organic matter before planting.

ACIDITY OR ALKALINITY

There is another aspect of your soil that you may need to take account of with some climbers: its relative acidity or alkalinity, usually expressed as the pH on a scale from 0 to 14. Soils with a pH above 7 are alkaline, those with a pH below 7, acid. Most soils are naturally between about pH 6 and pH 7.5 (more or less neutral) and most climbers will thrive in these conditions. But there are exceptions. Clematis prefer slightly alkaline conditions and they will be unlikely to grow well if you have a strongly acid, peaty soil which can't easily be changed without continuing effort. The pH of a slightly acid soil can be raised fairly simply, however, by adding lime and this is well worth doing before planting clematis in such conditions. There are rather fewer climbers that require acid conditions (and most of them are somewhat tender) which is just as well, for you can't easily decrease the pH of a naturally alkaline soil and I suggest that in these circumstances, you choose from some of the many species that *will* thrive in your soil.

DAMAGE TO WALLS AND BUILDINGS

The question of possible damage to the foundations of walls and buildings by the roots of climbers is often raised, but it is a fear that is easily dispelled. The very fact that climbers, even large ones, have proved themselves effective for so long in this role is testimony to their safety. The relative impact of a plant on foundations is a reflection of its water demand. Plants with a high water demand such as weeping willows or poplars take a great deal of water from the soil and, on sites with a high clay content, can be responsible for shrinkage and general changes in volume of the clay during wet and dry periods. This, in turn, causes stresses and damage to foundations. All garden climbers have low water demands and therefore have little effect on the soil water content, even on fairly heavy clays.

Tropaeolum majus **is best grown in poor soil**

TREATMENTS FOR COMMON PEST AND DISEASE PROBLEMS ON CLIMBERS

Problem	Treatment	Problem	Treatment
Aphids	Use a proprietary contact insecticide; pick off affected shoots by hand or wash insects off with hose.	Millepedes	Dust in affected area with derris.
Beetles	Normally, treatment is not necessary or justified but in cases of extensive attack use a proprietary contact insecticide.	Rabbits	The only sure protection is to use a wire netting fence with the lower edge turned outwards at 90° over the soil surface.
Birds	Erect netting or other protection; in really severe cases, erect bird scarers but remember that all birds enjoy legal protection and may not be harmed.	Red spider mites	No treatment is really feasible, although keeping plants well watered and mulched will help limit the impact of attacks.
Canker	Cut out and destroy affected branches; no chemical treatment is possible.	Root pests	Normally, no treatment is feasible but with severe and persistent attacks, dust around affected plants with derris or other soil insecticide.
Capsid bugs	The insects are too unpredictable and erratic in occurrence to make any treatment feasible.	Root disease	Destroy severely affected plants.
Caterpillars	Pick off by hand if the caterpillars can be found and are present in small numbers. If masses of insects occur, pick off and destroy entire affected leaves or use a proprietary contact insecticide.	Rust	Spray with penconazole fungicide.
		Scale insects	Spray or drench with systemic insecticide.
Coral spot	Cut away and destroy affected branches or twigs, cutting well into the healthy wood. On valuable ornamental plants, then spray the surrounding branches with a systemic fungicide.	Slugs	Use proprietary slug pellets or liquid controls, or home-made remedies such as traps baited with beer. Surround the base of plants with fine powders, such as ash or soot, or a low barrier of finely spiny twigs such as gorse.
Fertilizer deficiency	Give liquid fertilizer.	Snails	If serious, use methods recommended for slugs but generally they are less serious, fewer in number and can be combated by collecting them by hand and by locating and eradicating them from their hiding places among climbing plants.
Fungal decay	Destroy affected parts; no other treatment is feasible.		
Gall	Normally no treatment is justified, but cut out if severely disfiguring.		
Grey mould	Destroy affected parts; spray with systemic fungicide.	Sooty mould	Wash off mould with water or destroy badly affected leaves and then identify and treat the insect pest responsible for forming the honey dew on which the mould grows.
Leaf hoppers	The insects are too erratic and unpredictable to make any treatment practicable.	Stem and foot rot	Little can be done but, as it is often associated with waterlogging, improve drainage of the affected area. If on sweet peas, be sure to rotate the growing position each year.
Leaf miners	Remove and destroy affected leaves on herbaceous climbers.		
Leaf spot	In most instances no treatment is necessary, for leaf spot diseases are rarely severe. Where attacks appear to be related to general poor growth, however, spray with systemic fungicide.	Virus	Effects are usually mild, so no treatment is necessary.
		Voles	Set mouse traps or use proprietary poison baits.
Mice	Set traps or use proprietary poison baits.	Whiteflies	No treatment is feasible on outdoor plants.
		Wilt disease	See page 26.
Mildew	Ensure that plants are not allowed to become too dry and apply systemic fungicide or sulphur.	Woodlice	Dust around plants with proprietary soil insecticide and locate and eradicate them from their hiding places.

PRUNING

In training a climber, you persuade it to grow in certain directions and to have its branches or stems arranged in a particular pattern. This serves the purposes of ensuring that it fits into its allotted space, that it grows effectively and efficiently, appears attractive and/or produces the optimum number of flowers or fruits. On pages 11 to 13, I show all of the commonest systems for training climbers, which in most instances are dictated by the types of support on which the plants grow. To some extent, successful training can be achieved by the manner in which the stems are tied to the supports, but in large measure, it is pruning that provides the means to the end.

But while pruning is an important part of training, it continues to serve a valuable and essential purpose even on mature and established climbers where the basic training has already been completed. Grapevines, for example, have usually been trained into their basic framework by the third year or so but they must continue to be pruned annually thereafter. I have given the pruning requirements of each type of climber under the individual entries but there are some important basic principles best described here.

STIMULATING GROWTH

Pruning involves cutting off parts of plants. Clearly, this reduces their size but, more importantly, it stimulates other parts to grow. The buds at the end or apex of a stem exert a chemical suppressing influence on other buds further down. This phenomenon is called apical dominance. Cut off the end of a stem, therefore, and those other buds, freed of chemical constraint, will burst into life. If they are leaf buds, you will have foliage further down the stem; if flower buds, then blossoms will arise from top to bottom. Quite commonly, some pruning away of the apex is usefully combined with simply bending the stem down to the horizontal, since this also helps to diminish apical dominance and stimulate more uniform flower and leaf production.

Cutting away a large proportion of a plant is called hard pruning; cutting away a little is called light pruning. In general, you should hard prune those plants that are the less vigorous growers. This is simply because, in stimulating bud development as I have described, pruning actually generates more growth.

HOW TO PRUNE

Regardless of the amount of stem to be removed, pruning cuts should always be made just above a bud, leaf, flower, branch fork or other actively growing structure, never in the middle of a stem or branch. This ensures that the cut surface heals quickly and doesn't merely wither and allow decay organisms to enter. On other than very slender stems, the cut should be sloped away from the bud or other organ, but must not be so close as to damage it – about 5mm (¼in) above is safe. And even on large woody stems, never apply a wound sealing compound. These were once considered to be of benefit to the plant but are now thought, at best, useless and, at worst, positively harmful.

WHEN TO PRUNE

I know that gardeners are generally even more puzzled by the matter of when to prune than how to prune but this too has a simple logic. Pruning time is related to flowering time and the manner in which the flowers are produced. Perennial climbers bear their flowers in one of two main ways – those that flower before mid-summer usually do so on shoots that grew during the previous season; those that flower after mid-summer usually do so on shoots produced during the current year. If you prune one of the former types early in the year you will cut off many of the current year's flower buds. The trick with climbers of this type is always to prune *after* flowering and to do so before much additional growth has taken place. Climbers that flower in the first half of the year should therefore be pruned immediately after the flowers fade, and they generally require light pruning. Those that flower in the second half of the year may be pruned immediately afterwards but are often better left until very early in the following season, and some among this group require rather harder pruning.

PRUNING TOOLS

Good pruning is best achieved with good tools, and no gardener can manage without a pair of secateurs or pruners. Choose between the single-bladed anvil pattern which is best for hard woody stems but tends to crush softer ones, and the two-bladed scissor or by-pass type which is less robust but more gentle in action. Ideally, have both. If you have large climbers with stout woody stems, you will also require a pair of loppers.

Clematis 'Jackmanii Superba', 'Victoria' and 'Comtesse de Bouchaud'

WALLS

Almost any type of wall will suffice, although it is as well to be sure that the mortar and the bricks or stonework are sound, especially if the wall is tall. Old and crumbly structures will crumble even more and though I confess to having a low and very old brick wall in my own garden that is actually held together by an 'Oro di Bogliasco' ivy, this isn't, in general, an approach that I recommend. Self-clinging climbers such as ivy need no means of attachment but for most others, horizontal wires positioned about 20-25cm (8-10in) apart offer the best solution. Use plastic coated wire specially intended for the purpose – wire that can be tensioned without snap-ping. For most climbers, wire 2mm (½in) thick will suffice and it is best attached to looped vine eyes, screwed into wall plugs. It is possible to buy unthreaded vine eyes for hammering into mortar, but in my experience they bend too easily and also have sharp edges that cut into the wire. For very large climbers needing stronger and more extensive wires, it is worth using straining bolts, correctly fitted onto angled brackets in order to tension the wires satisfactorily. The stems may be secured to the wires by thinner, more pliable wire or with garden twine – but do check all ties at least once each year to be certain they aren't too tight.

A large, mature and woody climber such as an established *Wisteria* is usu-ally too irregular in shape and also too heavy to tie onto wires, and is better secured with individual vine eyes, placed where convenient. Lead-headed nails are often advocated but I am unimpressed; they are expensive, not strong enough to hold any other than very flimsy stems and, in any event, clamp the plant too tightly to the wall, allowing no flow of air beneath and behind it.

TRELLIS

For lightweight plants with irregular and extensive growth, trellis offers another way of attaching a climber to a wall. It also has the merit of provid-ing a fairly attractive wall covering even when the climber itself may be leafless and bare. But it is important to attach it to 2.5cm (1in) thick battens in order to raise it from the wall surface, and important also to select a type of trellis that is strong enough

Hydrangeas and roses against a house

Lonicera x italica **on a trellis**

for the purpose. Some of the rather appealing diamond-patterned wooden trellis is too flimsy to be of much use with any other than very small plants, while many of the very durable plastic clematis nettings are scarcely things of beauty, so choose carefully.

Provided it is intrinsically strong enough, a trellis is a very versatile support for climbing plants. Wooden, square-sectioned trellis can be most effective when attached, rather in the manner of a wooden fence panel, to two posts sunk 45cm (18in) or so into the ground. It can thus act as a screen, partitioning one part of the garden from another or concealing some unsightly object. Where you have the choice; orientate the trellis in a warm and sunny position rather than a cool and shady one to obtain the most uniform exposure to sunshine. Smaller trellis sections, 30cm (12in) or so tall, may be fixed to the top of a fence or even a wall to enable climbers to be trained horizontally. Do be sure to use very strong trellis for this purpose, however, and secure it firmly. And be sure, also, that any fence to which it is fixed is also stoutly anchored, because the additional height and wind resistance of the climbers themselves could cause instability.

Trellis can also be used very effectively as infilling panels for open framework arches, arbours, summerhouses, small pavilions and low fences. And in all of these situations, climbers may be planted to scramble over it. Yet again, I must stress the importance of using strong, robust trellis made from durable timber that really will still be standing when your

climbers are mature. Remember, too, that while a painted wooden structure can be most attractive, it will only be really practical if it is clothed with a climber that requires fairly strict annual pruning. Otherwise, the whole structure becomes impossible ever to repaint and begins to look simply shabby.

ARCHWAYS

I am a firm advocate of the value of archways in gardens. Positioned over path corners or used as focal points, they can play an invaluable role in adding interest to the garden and helping to divide it up into discrete areas, each with its own character. But an archway without climbers is cake without the icing, and they provide the most wonderful opportunities for you to increase your collection of climbing plants. Purpose-built archways are obtainable made from metal, usually painted or plastic coated, and these are generally best in a more formal garden. Wooden structures are most appropriate for rural settings but whether the wood used is planed timber, or (and better I think) round rustic poles, it should have been pressure treated with preservative. Vertical posts should be sunk 45-60cm (18-24in) in the ground and rammed in hard without concreting. All angles should be braced with diagonals.

PERGOLAS

A pergola sounds very grand but, in fact, is nothing more than an open framework for the support of climbers. The very finest pergolas, admittedly, have brick pillars and wooden cross-pieces but perfectly acceptable versions for smaller gardens are built entirely from wood, applying much the same criteria as for an archway. The main danger when constructing a pergola is that insufficient attention is paid to its lateral support and the whole is built in a single very long run, and thus has inherent instability. Arranging for the pergola to include at least one right-angled turn will help it structurally.

PILLARS

The pillar is the simplest of all climbing plant supports, being a single upright structure around which the climber is tied and trained. The commonest, and in many ways most practical and attractive pillars, are lengths of hardwood tree trunk, about 2m (6-7ft) tall and sunk firmly into the ground. It is essential, however, to use a durable hardwood, such as oak, otherwise the base will rot and render the whole thing unstable just at the moment when your climber reaches maturity.

TRIPODS

The tripod is, I think, the most under-used and under-appreciated of climbing plant supports, although they are seen commonly enough in large public

Clematis montana **'Elizabeth' grows best with its top in full sun**

gardens and can easily be copied. The ideal height for a tripod is about 1.5m (5ft) and, once again, I think rustic poles are the most appealing constructional material. In more formal gardens, however, you might want to be really adventurous and produce some of the painted box-type obelisk structures so popular in Tudor and Medieval times.

OTHER PLANTS

I have already explained that naturally, climbers tend to climb on each other or on other plants to gain their support and this same process can be imitated in gardens, although with caution. It is important always to choose plants of complementary vigour: a climber that grows 3m (10ft) in a season is an inappropriate choice to scramble over a shrub only 1m (3ft) tall, and a very vigorous perennial climber can cause harm to a relatively young tree. Both evergreen and deciduous support plants may be used – the brilliant red perennial *Tropaeolum* or a small-flowered *Clematis*, for instance, looks particularly attractive when growing over or through a dark-leaved conifer or similar evergreen.

Some small clematis can also look very pretty when threading their way through heathers, whereas others look better cascading down from the branches of a low tree. On trees with fairly long clear lengths of trunk, some tying in will almost certainly be necessary to assist the climber to reach the lowest limbs, but thereafter no further artificial help should be needed.

It is when dead trees or stumps are used as support for climbers, however, that the greatest problems can arise. An entire dead tree will very soon become unstable, an instability hastened by the growth of a climber on it. Unless it is a very durable hardwood such as an oak, the wood will decay after a few years and a gale can bring the entire structure, climber and all, crashing to the ground. Cutting the tree down to leave a length of stump over which a climber is grown may minimize the likely physical damage if it falls, but frustration will still ensue at the loss of an important garden feature. And in the case of non-coniferous trees, a dead stump can easily act as a focus for infection of the site by honey fungus, with disastrous consequences for the garden as a whole.

Wisteria **growing over a pergola**

The two common species of *Actinidia* make up a valuable and contrasting pair of deciduous, twining woody climbers from eastern Asia. The best known ornamental species is *Actinidia kolomikta* but several others bear edible fruits and it is to this group that *A. deliciosa* (still sometimes called *A. chinensis*) belongs. It is better known as the Chinese gooseberry or, since it became such an important crop plant in New Zealand, the Kiwi fruit.

Actinidia kolomikta

SITE AND SOIL Against a sunny, warm wall in well prepared soil, preferably a rich, moisture-retentive loam with no tendency to drying out or waterlogging. Very hardy, tolerates at least -20°C (-4°F) in winter.
SIZE 2m (6ft) after three years, up to 6-7m (20-23ft) eventually if unpruned.
PROPAGATION Easy, from semi-ripe cuttings or layering.

❝ There are few more arresting sights than the foliage colours of a well grown Actinidia kolomikta *but the plant must have full sun on a warm sheltered wall for them to develop fully and I find they generally appear about two or three years after planting. The pattern really is special – the basic colour of the heart-shaped leaves is pale green but the ends look as though they have been dipped in white emulsion paint and then, after a day or two, a pink tinge appears and eventually a large part of the leaf becomes a quite deep rosy pink. In autumn, they turn an attractive red. On established plants, small fragrant white flowers appear in early summer. ❞*

Actinidia kolomikta

CARE

Although it will grow through trees, it is more satisfactorily trained against horizontal support wires on a brick or stone wall. Mulch in late autumn and again in spring, preferably with leaf mould. Give a balanced general fertilizer in spring.

PROPAGATION

See *Actinidia deliciosa*.

PRUNING

Cut out any straggly or untidy stems in summer and then in winter, tie in any side-shoots required to extend the framework and prune all remaining side-shoots back to about 5cm (2in) from their junction with the main framework.

PROBLEMS

Apart from fruit pests, such as aphids and caterpillars on *Actinidia deliciosa*, both species are fairly trouble-free.

✳ **STRIKING AND UNUSUAL FOLIAGE**
✳ **NOT TOO VIGOROUS**
✳ **FRAGRANT FLOWERS**
✳ **EXTREMELY HARDY**

Actinidia deliciosa

SITE AND SOIL Against a sunny, warm and sheltered wall in well prepared soil, preferably a rich, moisture-retentive loam which has no tendency for drying out or waterlogging. Moderately hardy, tolerates -15°C (5°F) in winter.
SIZE Unpruned, will reach 30m (100ft) or more, but ideally pruned for fruiting on a wall about 2-3m (6-10ft) high and 3-4m (10-13ft) wide.
PROPAGATION Easy, from semi-ripe cuttings or layering.

❝ *One of the most vigorous climbing plants I have ever seen in Britain was a specimen of* Actinidia deliciosa *that had been grown from one of the original seeds first brought here from China in 1900. Shoots from this single plant reached at least 15 and probably 20m (50-60ft) into the tops of nearby trees. The leaves are correspondingly large with bristly margins. Nonetheless, if you prune carefully and grow it in a warm position, it will reward you with a crop of its uniquely flavoured fruits although you must be sure that you have the self-fertile variety or grow two separate male and female plants.* ❞

CARE

You will usually be sold a pair comprising a male and female, quite commonly grown in the same pot. They should be planted as one but their shoots trained in opposite directions against a sheltered wall and tied in to firmly anchored horizontal wires.

Actinidia deliciosa fruits

Occasionally, it may be possible to obtain a female plant onto which a male branch has been grafted. Mulch in late autumn and again in spring with well rotted manure or garden compost. Give a light dressing of sulphate of potash in early spring with a balanced general fertilizer about a month later. When fruiting, give a liquid feed every two weeks or so during summer. To fruit well, they require a cold spell in winter, then about eight months reliably free from frost with warmth in late summer.

PROPAGATION

Take semi-ripe cuttings of the current year's shoots in late summer and strike them in a 50:50 mixture of sand and peat in a shaded frame or propagator, using bottom heat of 25°C (77°F) if conditions are cool. They should root within six months. Alternatively, layer low-growing branches. If seed is set, it may be sown fresh in a sand-peat mixture in clay pans and left outdoors overwinter. Irregular germination should occur in about six months but seedlings of *Actinidia deliciosa* usually turn out to be male.

PRUNING

In the first and second seasons, form a permanent framework by tying-in the main shoot vertically and the lateral shoots horizontally, cutting them off at the tips when they have filled their allotted space. Sub-laterals will arise from the laterals and these should be pinched back just above five leaves from their base and any side-shoots that then develop should be pinched out. In the third season, fruits should be formed on the sub-laterals each of which should be cut off at a point six or seven leaves beyond the fruit. Side-shoots will then arise from the sub-laterals but these should be pinched out as before. The fruits are ripe when they yield under firm thumb pressure and should then be picked by snapping them off from their stalks. Late in each winter, cut back the fruiting sub-laterals to a point two buds beyond where the fruit was borne and once the plant is properly established, cut out completely the oldest third of the sub-laterals so they are renewed on a three-year cycle. It should not be necessary to renew the permanent framework of main shoots and laterals.

✻ **EDIBLE FRUITS**
✻ **VIGOROUS GROWTH**
✻ **SIMILAR HARDINESS TO GRAPEVINES**

RECOMMENDED VARIETIES
Self-fertile (one plant only needed): 'Blake', 'Jenny'; Female: 'Hayward' (generally the best for temperate climates). When buying a male plant, it is likely to be the variety 'Tomuri' or given a title such as 'All Purpose'.

AKEBIA

Akebia quinata
Chocolate Vine

SITE AND SOIL Tolerant of most aspects but particularly reliable against cool and shady walls. Requires well prepared soil to establish, preferably a rich, moisture-retentive loam. Fairly hardy, tolerates -10°C (14°F) in winter.
SIZE 2m (6-7ft) after three years, up to 10-12m (33-40ft) eventually.
PROPAGATION Fairly easy, from semi-ripe cuttings or layering.

66 This is a very vigorous but highly distinctive oriental climber for less formal situations. The twining stems will wrap themselves around any support, although one of the most impressive specimens I have seen was simply a huge mound of growth covering an old tree stump. In mild areas or warm winters, Akebia *will be more or less evergreen but is usually thought of as a deciduous species. The five-'fingered' leaves are pretty enough but it is the flowers that will cause comment in spring. The males and females are separate but on the same inflorescence – the females towards the base and 2-3cm (1in) wide, the males towards the tip and much smaller, but all strikingly coloured deep purple and with a spicy perfume. Occasionally, in warm summers, fruits are produced, looking for all the world like greyish-purple coloured sausages. 99*

Akebia quinata

CARE
Minimal training but robust support – an old tree, a large and stout pergola or a tall wall will suffice. Although hardy when established, young plants will benefit from some protection, especially in their first winter. Mulch in late autumn and again in spring, preferably with garden compost or leaf mould. Give a balanced general fertilizer in spring until established; little feeding is needed thereafter. Once established, they are best left undisturbed and for this reason it is wise to buy a container-grown plant.

PROPAGATION
Take semi-ripe cuttings of the current year's shoots in late summer and strike them in a 50:50 mixture of sand and peat in a shaded frame or propagator, using bottom heat of 25°C (77°F) if conditions are cool. They should root within six months.

SIMILAR SPECIES
Akebia trifoliata is seen sometimes. It is similar to *A. quinata* but has three-lobed, always deciduous leaves and flowers less reliably. It is also more likely to be damaged by late frosts.

Alternatively, layer low-growing branches. If seed is available, sow it in a sand and loam mixture in clay pans and leave outdoors overwinter.

PRUNING
Little needed but very vigorous, and overgrown plants may be cut back hard in spring and will regenerate satisfactorily.

PROBLEMS
None.
* **UNUSUALLY COLOURED FRAGRANT FLOWERS**
* **VERY VIGOROUS**
* **SUITABLE FOR DIFFICULT SITUATIONS**

Ampelopsis glandulosa var. brevipedunculata

SITE AND SOIL In full sun against a tall wall or other robust support in well prepared moisture-retentive soil. Very hardy, tolerates at least -20°C (-4°F) in winter.
SIZE Eventually, in good conditions, will reach 8m (25ft) although the real size is seldom apparent for the stems flop down over their supporting structure.
PROPAGATION Fairly easy, from semi-ripe cuttings, seed or by layering.

❝ *This is a distinctive climber with large three- or rarely five-lobed, rather hop-like leaves and markedly hairy young shoots. Despite its lush foliage, however, the real glory of the plant doesn't become apparent until early in the autumn when the insignificant greenish flowers give way to vivid blue fruits. There are few more stunning sights in a large garden than a mature specimen of one of these magnificent climbers when, after a hot summer, it bears a rich crop of berries which the full autumn sun catches and throws into contrast against the seasonal foliage colours.* ❞

CARE

Plant in full sun to be sure of obtaining the best fruit set – against a large sunny and sheltered wall is ideal or over a summerhouse in a sunny position. Although this is a tendril climber, it is often unable to support

A particularly attractive Asian group of deciduous tendril climbers, closely related to *Vitis* and also to *Parthenocissus* which differs in having self-clinging suckers. Nonetheless, some species have been moved from one genus to the other and may be found under different names in different nurseries. They are all fairly vigorous and not really suitable plants for small gardens.

RECOMMENDED VARIETIES

'Elegans' is a variety more familiar as an indoor pot plant. Not surprisingly, it is much less vigorous and its appeal lies in the leaf variegation of pink and white. It is also much less hardy and is a classic example of the weakness of variegated varieties – outdoors, it must have the shelter of a warm wall in a mild area for it barely tolerates more than a few degrees of winter frost. The form *citrulloides* has very deeply and narrowly five-lobed leaves.

its own weight when mature, and a cradle of strategically placed wires will be needed. Mulch in late autumn and spring with leaf mould or garden compost. Give a light dressing of a balanced general fertilizer in spring.

PROPAGATION

Take semi-ripe cuttings of the current year's shoots in late summer and strike them in a 50:50 mixture of sand and peat in a shaded frame or propagator, using bottom heat of 25°C (77°F) if conditions are cool. The cuttings should root within six months. If seed is set, it should be sown fresh in sand, or sand and loam mixture in clay pans and left outdoors overwinter. Irregular germination should occur in about six months.

PRUNING

Little is needed although extremely

A. g. brevipedunculata 'Elegans'

vigorous plants may be cut back hard in late winter or early spring and will regenerate. Alternatively, establish a regular pruning regime by forming a basic framework and pruning all side-shoots back to within 5cm (2in) of this framework in early spring. This approach will be essential in a confined space but does mean a continuing committment to a great deal of work.

PROBLEMS

Usually none although mildew can occur in hot dry summers.

✳ **HIGHLY ATTRACTIVE BLUE BERRIES**
✳ **VERY VIGOROUS GROWTH**
✳ **LARGE LEAVES WITH GOOD AUTUMN COLOUR**

ARISTOLOCHIA

There is only one common and familiar twining species of *Aristolochia* in the shape of *A. macrophylla* (still often seen under its older name of *A. durior*), but this is a very large genus indeed, ranging from native herbs to tropical climbers of great vigour. Many are too tender for outdoor cultivation but a few certainly deserve to be better known.

Aristolochia macrophylla

Aristolochia macrophylla

SITE AND SOIL In a sheltered but preferably sunny position in well prepared soil, preferably a rich, moisture-retentive loam with no tendency to drying out. Hardy, tolerates -20°C (-4°F) in winter.
SIZE 3m (10ft) after three years, up to 9m (30ft) eventually.
PROPAGATION Easy, by division.

❛❛ I have seen pipes smoked by Dutchmen and I must confess that none of them greatly resembled the early summer flowers of the North American Aristolochia macrophylla, *but that's the inventiveness of botanists for you. In practice, the curiously bent flowers are formed by the inflated yellowish-green and brown calyx, for there are no true petals. But even*

without the flowers, the plant is worth growing for its most attractive rather pale green heart-shaped leaves. It is vigorous and also quick-growing so makes a useful cover for unsightly buildings or other structures. Although the flowers of many tropical species have an unpleasant smell, the aroma here is fairly agreeable and comes predominantly from the bark. ❜❜

CARE
Train on horizontal support wires against a tall wall or, more effectively and simply, over a pergola, small building or arbour. Good soil is essential and this must not be allowed to dry out so mulch in late autumn and, most importantly, again in spring, preferably with compost or leaf mould rather than animal manures. Give a balanced general fertilizer in spring.

PROPAGATION
Easiest by division but also by softwood cuttings in spring in a 50:50 sand and peat mixture with bottom heat of about 25°C (77°F).

PRUNING
None necessary but cut out any straggly or untidy shoots after flowering in summer.

PROBLEMS
None.

✳ **UNUSUAL FLOWERS**
✳ **RAPID GROWTH**
✳ **PLEASANTLY FRAGRANT**

Aristolochia sempervirens

SIMILAR SPECIES
Aristolochia sempervirens (syn. *altissima*) is a rare but intriguing evergreen climber from the Mediterranean, suitable for a plantsman's mild garden or a large conservatory. It has heart-shaped glossy green leaves and strangely inflated yellowish-brown spring flowers with conspicuous dark lines. It seems to occur in two forms, the more tender being a climber that will eventually reach about 5m (16ft), while the more hardy is a scrambling, ground-covering plant. Cultivation and propagation are as for *A. macrophylla*.

Berberidopsis corallina
Coral Plant

SITE AND SOIL In a protected situation with shelter; tolerant of most aspects, including cool and shady provided it is protected from drying winds. Preferably in moist but not waterlogged soil that is at least slightly acidic. Fairly hardy, tolerates -10°C (14°F) in winter but must not have wind exposure.
SIZE 1m (3ft) after two years, up to 4-5m (13-16ft) eventually.
PROPAGATION Fairly easy, from semi-ripe cuttings or layering.

" It's a curious fact that some of the most spectacular and stunning of garden plants, especially those from South America, belong to one-species genera. This evergreen scrambling and twining climber is one of them although its name shouldn't mislead you into thinking it is related to Berberis. Unfortunately, it has another common South American characteristic in that it is difficult to satisfy its requirements in a temperate garden. But it is well worth the effort of trying for its lush, serrated leaves and its small, spherical flowers which hang like bunches of fragile cherries and are almost as long-lived through the summer as fuchsias. "

CARE

In mild areas, this plant is best trained in a semi-natural woodland setting, up a post or tree; in less mild regions, train it against horizontal

Berberidopsis corallina

support wires on a warm wall. Mulch in late autumn and again in spring with garden compost or leaf mould, not animal manures. Give a balanced general fertilizer in spring.

PROPAGATION

Layer in autumn or take semi-ripe cuttings of the current year's shoots in late summer and strike them in a 50:50 mixture of sand and peat in a shaded frame or propagator, using bottom heat of 25°C (77°F) if conditions are cool. They should root within six months. Seed is rarely and unsatisfactorily set in temperate gardens but if good imported seed is available, it should be sown in a sand and peat mixture in clay pans and left outdoors overwinter. Irregular germination should occur within about six months.

PRUNING

On established plants, the growth becomes congested so cut out any straggly or untidy stems in spring and again if necessary in late summer.

PROBLEMS
None.
✳ **UNUSUAL AND BEAUTIFUL FLOWERS**
✳ **EVERGREEN**
✳ **LONG FLOWERING SEASON**

BIGNONIA

Bignonia capreolata
Cross Vine

SITE AND SOIL Warm, sunny position with shelter. Requires well prepared and rich, moisture-retentive loam. Barely hardy, tolerates -5°C (23°F) in winter.
SIZE 2m (6ft) after three years, up to 9-15m (30-50ft) eventually in favourable conditions.
PROPAGATION Easy, by layering.

❝ *There are unfortunately very few members of the tropical family Bignoniaceae that can be considered hardy in temperate climates.* Bignonia *and* Campsis *(page 21) are among the very best of them. The rich scarlet and orange flower trumpets of the tendril climber* Bignonia *are characteristic of the family and in an appropriately mild area, this will make an absolutely stunning display in early summer. If you are fortunate, they will be followed by thin, flattened, rather bean-like pods. Although evergreen in the mildest areas (and especially when grown as a ground cover), it may lose at least some of its leaves in cold winters. You will search in vain for the origin of the common name until you start to prune it, when a dark cross-like marking is apparent in the wood.* ❞

Tecoma capensis (syn.Tecomaria capensis)

CARE
Use strong horizontal support wires against a tall sunny wall. Even in mild areas, give protection to young plants in their first winter. In very rich soil, it may be difficult to induce flowering and it may be best in such circumstances to confine the roots. Mulch in late autumn and in spring, with garden compost or leaf mould. Give a balanced rose or other flowering-shrub fertilizer in spring.

PROPAGATION
Layer low-growing shoots in late autumn or winter.

PRUNING
Prune in spring, when any winter frost and cold damage will be apparent. Cut out all damaged shoots and, in confined situations such as against a wall, cut back all of the previous season's growth by between a half and two-thirds, depending on the overall vigour.

SIMILAR SPECIES
Tecoma capensis (Cape Honeysuckle) is an evergreen twining relative of *Bignonia* from southern Africa, similarly tender and with clusters of beautiful trumpet-shaped scarlet flowers. Although really more reliable in a conservatory or greenhouse, it is well worth trying in a sheltered spot in really mild areas where it will reach around 4-5m (13-16ft) in about five years.

PROBLEMS
None, although when grown in conservatories, very prone to both whiteflies and mealy bugs.
✳ **SPECTACULARLY EXOTIC FLOWERS**
✳ **FAIRLY EASY TO GROW IN MILD AREAS**
✳ **OFTEN SUCCESSFUL IN POORER SOILS**

Campsis radicans
Trumpet Vine

SITE AND SOIL A warm, sunny or very lightly shaded position with shelter. Requires well prepared and rich, moisture-retentive loam. Hardy, tolerates -20°C (-4°F) in winter.
SIZE 2m (6ft) after three years, up to 9m (30ft) eventually.
PROPAGATION Easy, by layering or cuttings.

❝ I think that this lovely plant must be the hardiest truly exotic looking climber that can be grown outdoors in a temperate climate. In favourable conditions, far from struggling in the way that so many warm climate plants do, it can be almost rampant. Typically the trumpet-shaped flower is orange and yellow but colour variants exist. It is deciduous and climbs and scrambles by means of aerial roots – some of the most effective specimens I have seen were, admittedly, in rather mild areas where they were clipped to form shaped bushes or hedges. ❞

In appearance, these are the classic warm climate climbers with their trumpet-shaped flowers and brilliant, gaudy colours. Despite their brilliance, they aren't, however, truly tropical and originate in warm parts of North America and eastern Asia and this enables them to be grown successfully in the milder parts of temperate regions.

Campsis radicans

CARE

It is important to cut back the above ground growth to within about 20cm (8in) of soil level immediately after planting to encourage shoot development. When grown against horizontal wires or other artificial supports, careful tying-in or even a wire cradle may be needed because the aerial roots are scarcely strong enough to support the mass of stems and foliage. The soil must not be allowed to dry out, so mulch in late autumn and again in spring, preferably with garden compost or leaf mould. Give a balanced rose or other flowering-shrub fertilizer in spring.

PROPAGATION

Layer low-growing shoots in late autumn or winter. Alternatively, take leaf-bud cuttings in early spring, just before the buds break or softwood cuttings in early summer and strike them in a 50:50 peat and sand mixture in a propagator with very gentle or no bottom heat. Suckers occur extensively and may be pulled off and potted-up complete with roots. If seed is available, it should be sown in autumn in sand in clay pans and left outside overwinter. It should then germinate in spring.

PRUNING

Once mature plants are growing in

CAMPSIS

Campsis x *tagliabuana* 'Madame Galen'

semi-natural situations, they may be allowed free rein but when trained against a wall, a permanent shoot framework should be established and side-shoots pruned to within 5cm (2in) of this framework in spring.

PROBLEMS

Campsis radicans is prone to a range of common pest and disease problems – whiteflies, mealy bugs, scale insects and mildew although never as severely outdoors as when grown as a conservatory plant.

✳ **BEAUTIFUL AND STRIKING FLOWERS**

✳ **LATE FLOWERING PERIOD**

✳ **FAIRLY HARDY**

Campsis grandiflora

Celastrus orbiculatus
Oriental Bittersweet

SITE AND SOIL Full sun or partial shade with any aspect. Requires well prepared and rich, moisture-retentive loam although with no tendency to waterlogging. Hardy, tolerates -20°C (-4°F) in winter.

SIZE Left unpruned, individual shoots will reach 5m (16ft) after three years, up to 12-15m (40-50ft) eventually but it usually forms a congested tangle over its support.

PROPAGATION Fairly easy, by layering or cuttings.

" *There is no more arresting sight in my garden in the chill days of late autumn than this deciduous twining climber from the colder parts of eastern Asia. Given space to accommodate its undoubted vigour, I have little hesitation in including it in my top three or four favourite, yet little known, climbing plants. In its summer foliage, I suppose it might be dismissed with a passing glance as little more than bindweed for although it has small flowers, they are greenish and fairly insignificant. Even the rounded pea-like fruits will, at first, produce little excitement. But then they ripen, darken and split open to expose a golden inner surface against which are set vivid scarlet seeds. Seen against the yellowing autumn foliage, this is horticultural jewellery of very special quality and the fruits then persist on the bare branches for many weeks as birds seem to neglect them.* "

CARE
A stout support is essential but the plant really needs no tying-in. Its stems twine very effectively of their own accord over fences, old trees, pergolas, summerhouses and similar structures. If the soil is rich and moist, no feeding should be necessary once the plant is established as it is naturally very vigorous.

PROPAGATION
With difficulty, I have managed to obtain successful layers in winter but root cuttings are generally considered the most reliable method. There is little point in raising plants

RECOMMENDED VARIETIES
Assuming that you have room for and want only one plant, it is essential to buy the unnamed hermaphrodite form in order to obtain the fruits.

from seed as they will be unisexual and non-fruiting.

PRUNING
Mature plants can be cut back more or less at will in early spring and will recover satisfactorily. In large gardens and over large supports moreover, they may be left unpruned.

PROBLEMS
None that I have encountered.

* **STUNNING WINTER APPEAL**
* **VIGOROUS**
* **HARDY**

Celastrus orbiculatus

CLEMATIS

As a genus, clematis needs no introduction, for its members are justifiably the most popular and widely known of all garden climbers. What is less generally appreciated, however, is the scope of the genus and the large number of attractive true species it contains to complement the wide range of large-flowered hybrids. Many of these species are also much easier to grow and more trouble free than their cultivated variants. Clematis belong, rather unexpectedly, to the buttercup family, Ranunculaceae, and occur throughout the temperate regions of the world. They climb by means of twining leaf stalks and most are deciduous, but many are partially and some fully evergreen. Most are also hardy outdoors in temperate areas, the exceptions lying mostly among the evergreen forms. The colour and form of their delightful flowers comes not from petals but mainly from petalloid sepals. Despite the existence of over 200 species and around 400 varieties and hybrids, clematis fall into several fairly well defined groups, the distinctions between them being important for the gardener, and it is into these groups that I have subdivided them here.

I have given general notes on the care, propagation and pruning of clematis on page 25-26 but for pruning purposes, they are divided into three main groups and their designation as Group 1, 2 or 3 is given with the account of each species or variety.

Clematis 'William Kennett'

CARE

The soil conditions required for all types of clematis are similar. They will always succeed best in fairly light but rich and slightly alkaline soil. Strongly acidic, impoverished or very heavy, wet and cold soils will result in poor growth. Although most will give some display in any aspect and all are best when the base of the plant is shaded, some types are undoubtedly better in certain positions. The evergreen forms and some of the less familiar late-flowering species require shelter and really must have the protection of a warm and sunny wall. The double and semi-double flowered types also need a warm, sunny and sheltered site. Many of the large-flowered, early hybrids give their best colours when the flowers are slightly shaded and for this reason, are often successful on a cool wall with little direct sun. The varieties of *Clematis alpina* and *C. macropetala*, too, are good plants for a more shaded situation.

Clematis are among the few plants for which deep planting is recommended. This is largely because many types are subject to a wilt disease (see page 26), and deep planting ensures that several leaf-bud nodes are below soil level and available, therefore, to renew growth if that above ground dies back. Plant with the soil level 15cm (6in) below the soil mark visible on the plant in its pot. Mulch all plants in late autumn and again in spring with well-rotted manure or garden compost. Give a top dressing with a balanced general fertilizer in early spring and preferably give liquid feed approximately

Clematis alpina sibirica **'White Moth' is one of the earliest flowering**

every three weeks during the summer.

Although there is a tendency for all types of clematis to be grown against house walls, more or less tied to plastic clematis netting, this is rarely the best method. Almost all of the more vigorous species and varieties are best grown in a semi-natural situation through old trees, over pergolas, archways or outbuildings. Some of the less vigorous late-flowering types that require Group 3 pruning are ideally trained through old shrub or climbing roses. And even those that are low enough in vigour and have sufficient appeal because of their continuous flowering to be trained against a wall are best tied to wooden trellis on battens rather than to plastic netting flush against the brickwork.

PROPAGATION

Not all clematis are equally easy to propagate. Most of the species can be grown fairly readily from seed, although selected forms will not necessarily come true to type, and some

decidedly inferior strains have found their way into commerce by this route. Once the seed is ripe, revealed by its 'hairs' becoming light and fluffy, it should be collected and sown promptly in seed pans, about 5mm (¼in) deep in a soil-based seedling compost and left outdoors or in a cold frame. Germination will be erratic and may take 12 months or even more.

Many types can be propagated by semi-ripe cuttings of the current year's shoots in late summer, but cuttings should be taken internodally – that is, the cut made midway between the nodal swellings, not just below one as is usual. This is because the highest concentration of root growth stimulating hormone occurs at the midway point. Trim the top of the cutting just above the node, cut off all except one leaf and push the cutting up to the node in a soil-based compost. Place the cuttings in a shaded frame or propagator, using bottom heat of about

25°C (77°F) if conditions are cool.

It isn't always appreciated that large clematis can be divided, much like herbaceous perennials, but this is always best done in late autumn when there is little likelihood of damage to the tender young shoots.

PRUNING

The three pruning groups are defined on the basis of flowering time but there is also some variation depending on the vigour of the variety. Group 1 types flower early in the year but on wood produced in the previous season. They should be pruned immediately after flowering by cutting back all weak and dead stems to just above a node to allow new growth to be produced. Any tangled or excessive growth should

also be cut back but large, well established plants that are growing where they may be allowed free rein need not be pruned. Conversely, a plant that has become a tangled mass (as many *Clematis montana* tend to) may be pruned back as hard as a Group 2 or a Group 3 plant and will regenerate successfully, although in the latter case, all of one year's flower buds will, of course, be removed.

Group 2 types flower early in the summer, also on the previous season's wood and should be pruned in early spring before new growth starts by cutting out any dead or weak stems and then cutting back the remainder by about 30cm (12in), to just above a pair of plump buds. Any dead leaf stalks should be trimmed

away and the plant generally tidied up.

Group 3 types flower late in the summer on the current year's wood and they should also be pruned early in the spring, but much more severely. All of the previous season's growth should be cut back to just above a pair of plump buds growing about 75cm (30in) above soil level. If there is so much top growth that it will be blown around in the winter winds, however, the bulk of it may be cut back in late autumn, leaving the final tidying until mid- to late winter.

PROBLEMS

Slugs and snails may be troublesome on young tender shoots as they emerge and mildew is sometimes a problem in hot seasons later in the summer. Apart from these, the major difficulty with clematis is a mysterious wilt disease. The cause is uncertain, although at least one species of pathogenic fungus may be involved but the symptoms are very evident – the top growth dies back, more or less to ground level and quite without warning or obvious reason. The species are much less likely to be affected than the hybrids. Affected plants should be cut back to just above soil level – the new growth that arises will often be unaffected. Should the problem persist, however, the affected plant should be dug up and disposed of. If another clematis is to be placed in the same spot, a hole of about 30 x 30 x 30cm (12 x 12 x 12in) should be dug and the soil replaced with fresh from elsewhere in the garden. The new plant should be planted deeply (see left) and preferably be a species rather than a large-flowered hybrid.

Clematis montana **will grow almost anywhere**

CLEMATIS Early-flowering species

Clematis alpina
(GROUP 1)

SITE AND SOIL Tolerant of all aspects but very good against cool shady walls. Moisture-retentive slightly alkaline soil. Very hardy, tolerates at least -20°C (-4°F) in winter.
SIZE 3-5m (10-16ft) after three or four years.
PROPAGATION Fairly easy, from semi-ripe cuttings in late summer, layering or seeds.

RECOMMENDED VARIETIES
'Burford White' (white), 'Columbine' (pale blue), 'Frances Rivis' (pale blue, large flowers), 'Frankie' (mid-blue with inner 'skirt'), 'Pamela Jackman' (deep blue), 'Rosy Pagoda' (pale pink), 'Ruby' (pink-purple), 'Willy' (pale pink, darker at base), ssp. *sibirica* 'White Moth' (double white).

Clematis alpina **'Willy'**

" *At one side of my front door is a climber whose flowers draw comment every spring from those who do not expect to find large, nodding, bell-shaped blooms of a rich blue on a plant whose foliage so clearly betrays it as a clematis. It is* Clematis alpina *and my plant is but one of a group of mainly white and blue flowered variants, all with delightful feathery seedheads, of this widespread species from the mountains of Europe and northern Asia.* "

* **NODDING, BELL-LIKE FLOWERS**
* **NOT VERY VIGOROUS**
* **ONE OF THE EARLIEST FLOWERING CLEMATIS**

C. alpina ssp. *sibirica* **'White Moth'**

Clematis alpina **'Ruby'**

Clematis macropetala 'Markham's Pink'

Clematis macropetala
(GROUP 1)

SITE AND SOIL Tolerant of all aspects but very good against cool shady walls. Moisture-retentive slightly alkaline soil. Very hardy, tolerates at least -20°C (-4°F) in winter.
SIZE 3-5m (10-16ft) after three or four years.
PROPAGATION Fairly easy, from semi-ripe cuttings in late summer, layering or seeds.

" *A Chinese species, similar in overall form to* Clematis alpina *but rather more vigorous, all of its varieties having semi-double flowers with slightly more flared bells. The two species complement each other perfectly and some of the loveliest plantings I know are where they are alternated along a wall or pergola.* "

RECOMMENDED VARIETIES
'Jan Lindmark' (purple-mauve, usually the earliest-flowering variety), 'Maidwell Hall' (deep blue), 'Markham's Pink' (pink).

EARLY-FLOWERING HYBRIDS OF *C. ALPINA* OR *C. MACROPETALA* TYPE
'Blue Bird' (blue-mauve), 'Helsingborg' (deep blue-purple, large flowers), 'Rosie O'Grady' (mauve-pink), 'White Swan' (white, large flowers).

✳ **NODDING, MORE OR LESS DOUBLE BELL-LIKE FLOWERS**
✳ **MODERATELY VIGOROUS**
✳ **ONE OF THE EARLIEST-FLOWERING CLEMATIS**

Clematis macropetala 'Jan Lindmark'

Clematis montana
(GROUP 1)

SITE AND SOIL Tolerant of all aspects including moderate shade but always best with its top in full sun. Not a plant for a house wall and best when allowed to grow over an old tree or out-building. Moisture-retentive, preferably slightly alkaline soil. Hardy, tolerates -20°C (-4°F) in winter.

SIZE 2-3m (6-10ft) after three years, up to 8m (25ft) eventually if unpruned.

PROPAGATION Easy, from semi-ripe cuttings in late summer or layering; not worth raising from seed because seedlings are of very variable quality.

> *I once owned a decrepit old brick garden shed alongside which someone had, many years previously, planted a clematis. It had a trunk like a tree and the building was virtually invisible beneath its all-embracing growth which, in late spring, was covered with a mass of pale mauve star-like flowers. That was* Clematis montana, *certainly the most popular and most loved clematis species and one of the best known of any type. It originates from China and the Himalayas, is vigorous and truly lovely and is now such an indispensible part of gardening that it is amazing to realize that it has been grown in cultivation for little more than 150 years. It must, however, be planted with circumspection in small gardens.*

RECOMMENDED VARIETIES

'Alexander' (white), 'Elizabeth' (pink, the best really strongly scented variety), 'Freda' (deep pink), f. *grandiflora* (white, scented, large flowers), 'Marjorie' (pink-cream), 'Mayleen' (deep pink, bronze foliage), 'Odorata' (pale pink, scented), 'Picton's Variety' (deep rose-pink, bronze foliage), 'Pink Perfection' (deep pink, scented), var. *rubens* (rose pink), var. *sericea* (white), 'Tetrarose' (pink-purple, large flowers), var. *wilsonii* (white, later-flowering into early summer).

* **MASSES OF OPEN, FOUR–'PETALLED' FLOWERS**
* **VERY VIGOROUS**
* **VERY HARDY**
* **WILL GROW ALMOST ANYWHERE**

Clematis montana 'Marjorie'

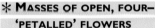

Clematis montana f. *grandiflora*

Clematis montana var. *rubens*

Clematis montana 'Continuity'

SIMILAR SPECIES

Clematis chrysocoma from southern China is a very pretty clematis, differing from *C. montana* in being less vigorous (no more than about 5m (16ft) eventually) but suitable for similar situations. White and pinkish flowered variants occur and a good and fairly common pink form called 'Continuity' may be derived from it.

Clematis x *vedrariensis* is an attractive pale rose-pink flowered hybrid between *C. montana* and *C. chrysocoma*. It will reach about 5m (16ft) but is rather less hardy. The two most commonly seen and best varieties are 'Highdown' and 'Rosea'.

Clematis montana 'Picton's Variety'

I always think of these beautiful plants as the most versatile of all garden clematis, for by selecting your varieties carefully, you can have a range of colours from white through mauves, pinks, reds and blues, some bicolours, many doubles and a principal flowering season in early summer but with the strong expectation of more blooms through the summer almost to early autumn. Most have large flowers of at least 15cm (6in) diameter and they are derived from one or more of three Chinese species, *Clematis florida, C. patens* and *C. lanuginosa.*

SITE AND SOIL Tolerant of most aspects but best when the bulk of the plant is in warm sun, against a sunny sheltered wall, although the flower colour is usually more intense if the head is in light shade. Moisture-retentive slightly alkaline soil. Hardy, tolerates -20°C (-4°F) in winter.
SIZE 2-3m (6-10ft) after three or four years.
PROPAGATION Difficult, especially from semi-ripe cuttings in late summer; layering is generally easier.

Florida Group
(GROUP 2)

CLEMATIS FLORIDA is a rare deciduous or semi-evergreen Chinese species that has passed its relatively low vigour and manageable proportions onto its progeny, most of which have double or semi-double flowers. They flower principally in late spring and early summer, most varieties having little repeat flowering later although, where this does occur, it is usually with single rather than double blooms.

Clematis **'Wada's Primrose'**

Clematis **'The President'**

RECOMMENDED VARIETIES
FLORIDA TYPES:
'Beauty of Worcester' (deep blue, double and single flowers), 'Belle of Woking' (silver-mauve, double), 'Duchess of Edinburgh' (white, double), 'Kathleen Dunford' (rose-purple, semi-double and single), 'Proteus' (mauve-pink, double, semi-double and single), 'Sylvia Denny' (white, semi-double and single), 'Vyvyan Pennell' (deep violet-blue, double, semi-double and single, probably the strongest growing among double-flowered clematis), 'Walter Pennell' (deep mauve-pink, semi-double and single).

Clematis **'Belle of Woking'**

Clematis 'Carnaby'

Patens and Lanuginosa Groups (GROUP 2)

'In many cases, it's now impossible to be sure which of these two species was more important in the development of any particular variety, although there is a crude rule of thumb that relates flowering time to origin.

CLEMATIS PATENS is a blue and white flowered species from China and Japan and its varieties tend to flower in late spring and early summer and then, like those of the Florida group, not usually again until the early autumn.

C. LANUGINOSA seems not to exist in the wild and was an old blue flowered Chinese garden plant. It gives rise to varieties that flower in late spring and early summer and then again, on and off through the summer.

I have divided my recommendations along these lines, therefore, and this should be of some guidance when making your selection. All are single-flowered unless I have indicated otherwise, and have appealing stamen colours of white, gold, brown or purple that contrast with the overall flower colour.

* **LARGE FLOWERS IN STUNNING COLOURS**
* **MODERATELY VIGOROUS**
* **CONSIDERABLE RANGE IN FLOWERING TIMES**

RECOMMENDED VARIETIES

PATENS TYPES:

'Alice Fisk' (pale blue), 'Barbara Dibley' (red with carmine bars), 'Barbara Jackman' (mauve-red with red bar), 'Bee's Jubilee' (mauve-pink with carmine bar), 'Corona' (deep purple, shaded pink), 'Daniel Deronda' (blue-violet, single and semi-double), 'Dr Ruppel' (deep rose-pink with darker bar), 'Gillian Blades' (white, wavy edges), 'Kathleen Wheeler' (mauve-purple), 'Lasurstern' (deep lavender-blue, wavy edges), 'Lincoln Star' (raspberry-pink), 'Lord Nevill' (deep blue, wavy edges), 'Miss Bateman' (white), 'Mrs N. Thompson' (deep purple-blue with scarlet bar), 'Richard Pennell' (blue-purple, very large flowers), 'The President' (deep blue-purple, an exception to the general rule in this group, flowering more or less all summer), 'Wada's Primrose' (creamy-yellow, an unusual colour, the closest to a real yellow among this type).

LANUGINOSA TYPES:

'Carnaby' (deep pink with darker bar), 'Crimson King' (crimson), 'Edith' (white), 'Elsa Späth' (blue-violet, purple shading), 'Haku-ôkan' (violet, single and semi-double), 'John Warren' (deep pink, darker edges), 'King Edward VII' (mauve with pink bar, very large flowers), 'Lady Northcliffe' (Wedgwood blue), 'Lawsoniana' (blue-mauve with pink flush), 'Lilacina Floribunda' (deep purple), 'Marie Boisselot' (white), 'Mrs Cholmondley' (lavender-blue), 'Nelly Moser' (mauve-pink with deep lilac bar, large flowers produced in abundance), 'Sealand Gem' (lavender with dark pink bar), 'Silver Moon' (silver-mauve), 'W. E. Gladstone' (lilac-blue), 'Will Goodwin' (lavender-blue, darker veins and wavy edges), 'William Kennett' (lavender-blue).

Jackmanii Group
(GROUP 3)

SITE AND SOIL Tolerant of most aspects but best when the bulk of the plant is in warm sun, although the flower colour is usually more intense if the head is in light shade. Best when grown over a fence, old tree, pergola or similar informal situation, rather than on a house wall. Moisture-retentive, preferably slightly alkaline soil. Hardy, tolerates -20°C (-4°F) in winter.

SIZE 2-3m (6-10ft) after three or four years.

PROPAGATION Difficult, especially from semi-ripe cuttings in late summer; layering is generally easier.

Clematis **'Hagley Hybrid'**

Clematis **'Jackmanii Superba'**

❝ *The most popular of all clematis varieties, 'Perle d'Azur', belongs to this group which contains a range of famous, much loved and undeniably beautiful plants with bold, large, generally single flowers in shades of red, pink, violet, blue and white. They are derived from a hybrid that arose in Jackman's nursery in Surrey, England in 1858 and is believed to have been a cross between* Clematis viticella *and* C. lanuginosa. *They flower reliably and more or less continuously from mid-summer until the early autumn but, unfortunately, I find that they aren't always positioned in the best place. Many gardeners grow them in the same manner as the early-flowering hybrids but they behave differently, and like most late summer-blooming shrubs, bear their flowers on stems produced during the current season. In consequence, the flowers tend to be borne towards the ends of rather long shoots which look delightful scrambling in a semi-wild manner but can form an untidy tangle when confined on a wall or trellis.* ❞

❋ **LARGE FLOWERS IN STUNNING COLOURS**

❋ **MODERATELY VIGOROUS**

❋ **CONTINUOUS FLOWERING FROM MID-SUMMER UNTIL AUTUMN**

Clematis viticella and its hybrids (GROUP 3)

SITE AND SOIL Tolerant of all aspects and on many types of support, but not very suitable for small house walls or trellis and best in a semi-natural situation. Moisture-retentive slightly alkaline soil. Hardy, tolerates -20°C (-4°F) in winter.
SIZE 4-5m (13-16ft) after three or four years.
PROPAGATION Relatively easy, from semi-ripe cuttings in late summer or layering.

Clematis 'Madame Julia Correvon'

Clematis 'Ville de Lyon'

C. viticella 'Purpurea Plena Elegans'

RECOMMENDED VARIETIES
'Abundance' (dark red), 'Alba Luxurians' (white with greenish tips), 'Ascotiensis' (blue, very large flowers for a viticella: up to 20cm (8in) in diameter), 'Blue Belle' (deep blue-purple), 'Duchess of Sutherland' (dark red), 'Etoile Violette' (purple), 'Huldine' (white), 'Kermesina' (dark red), 'Little Nell' (cream-white with pink flush), 'Madame Julia Correvon' (dark red), 'Margot Koster' (reddish-pink), 'Minuet' (cream with lilac edges), 'Mrs Spencer Castle' (pink, semi-double and single), 'Polish Spirit' (blue-purple), 'Royal Velours' (deep purple), 'Södertälje' (deep pink); 'Venosa Violacea' (white with purple veins), 'Ville de Lyon' (crimson), *Clematis viticella* (mauve-purple in the true species, but it is a variable plant so be sure to see yours in flower before you buy), 'Purpurea Plena Elegans' (violet-purple, double).

❝ *Growing through a beautiful old Victorian white climbing rose close to my main gate is a clematis that probably provokes more remark than any other plant in my garden. From mid-summer onwards, it is covered in deep velvety-red flowers that contrast magnificently with the blooms of the rose. The clematis is called 'Mme Julia Correvon' and it is one of the invaluable varieties derived from a southern European species called* Clematis viticella. *They are only moderately vigorous and therefore readily manageable. They generally have single, uncomplicated and slightly nodding flowers in reds, purples, blues and white. In most instances the flowers are small, up to about 7-8cm (3in) in diameter and, cascading down from the branches of a low tree, they are quite superb; as you look up at them, they seem to peer back and return your appreciation.* ❞

✳ **USUALLY SMALL, DAINTY FLOWERS WITH SOME LOVELY DEEP REDS**
✳ **MODERATELY VIGOROUS**
✳ **PARTICULARLY EFFECTIVE WITH SHRUB OR CLIMBING ROSES**

As summer wears on, a large range of rather different and individual clematis species begins to come into its own. Their foliage is often finely dissected and almost fern-like. Their flowers are generally much smaller and rather different in form from the summer-blooming types. Many are dainty and bell-shaped and all tend to look their best when growing informally through old trees or over small outbuildings. They fall naturally into several discrete groups, of which one of the most important comprises *Clematis tangutica* from China and two other closely related oriental species often confused with each other, *C. tibetana* from Tibet and *C. orientalis* from a wide area of eastern Europe and western Asia.

Clematis tangutica
(GROUP 3)

SITE AND SOIL Tolerant of all aspects but unsuited to restricted situations, such as against low walls. Very effective when grown through trees. Moisture-retentive slightly alkaline soil. Hardy, tolerates -20°C (-4°F) in winter.

SIZE Once established, will grow to 3-4m (10-13ft) each year, even with hard pruning. Unpruned, will eventually reach 5-6m (16-20ft).

PROPAGATION Easy, from semi-ripe cuttings in late summer, layering or seeds.

Clematis tangutica

❝ *Expert growers and breeders of most types of garden flower always seem to want a colour that doesn't exist. And those who specialize in early, large-flowered clematis varieties crave yellow. I never know why they bother, for there already exist within the genus some of the loveliest yellows in the plant kingdom; if only they would wait until after midsummer when the flowers of the Chinese* Clematis tangutica *and its allies are open. Depending on the species and variety, the bell-like flowers range in colour from pale yellow to the richest orange.*

These aren't, however, plants for the small courtyard garden as, although they should be hard pruned each year, the amount of growth that can be produced within a single season is quite prodigious. ❞

✻ **NODDING, BELL-LIKE YELLOW FLOWERS**
✻ **VIGOROUS**
✻ **VERY EASY TO GROW**

Clematis tangutica

RECOMMENDED VARIETIES

There has been change and confusion over the naming of the three main species of these clematis in recent years and, depending on the age of the catalogue (or the nurseryman), you may well find *Clematis tangutica* listed as *C. orientalis*, *C. tibetana* not listed at all, and almost any of the varieties under any of the species. The true *C. orientalis* is, however, a relatively unattractive species with rather dingy green-yellow flowers.

Clematis tangutica (golden-yellow flowers), *C. tangutica* 'Gravetye Variety' (yellow, vigorous and free flowering), *C. tangutica* 'Lampton Park' (yellow, large flowers). 'Aureolin' (yellow, very prolific), 'Burford Variety' (yellow), 'Corry' (lemon-yellow, large, wide open flowers), and 'Bill Mackenzie' (one of the best of all, very large, yellow flowers) are all probably hybrids involving *C. tangutica*. *C. tibetana* (greenish-yellow-orange flowers that tend to open out as they mature), *C. tibetana* ssp. *vernayi* exists under this name and also in four variants, of which the two commonest are 'Orange Peel' and 'LS & E 13342'* (remarkable rich yellow-orange flowers with markedly thickened sepals; all types are sometimes sold as 'orange peel clematis').

Clematis rehderiana

Clematis akebioides

SIMILAR SPECIES

Clematis rehderiana (pale yellow) is probably the commonest of the remaining yellow flowered oriental species but is very vigorous, reaching 8m (25ft) or more, and therefore best in larger gardens. *Clematis serratifolia* (yellow, markedly star-like flowers, free flowering), from China and Korea, is a pretty species with lush, bright green foliage that should be grown more widely; it tends to retain its flowers for a rather shorter time into the autumn than its relatives.

Clematis aethusifolia (pale yellow, bell-shaped flowers) is a delightful and rather less vigorous plant – about 2m (6ft) – from China with very delicate, ferny leaves. It tends to flower rather later than the other species and, being less vigorous, is well suited to smaller gardens and almost restrained enough to grow in a container.

Clematis akebioides (yellow or greenish-yellow flowers with darker outer surfaces) is another vigorous southern Chinese species, reaching 5m (16ft), and with a mass of dainty flowers.

* LS & E 13342 This curious name is no more than the collection number given to the plant by the collectors Ludlow, Sherriff and Elliott who first introduced it from the Himalayas in 1947. It is an unusual instance of a wild collection that proved subsequently to be a very good garden variety and yet, for some reason, was never named.

Clematis texensis
(GROUP 3)

SITE AND SOIL Tolerant of all aspects and suitable for growing against walls, on trellis, through and over shrubs and small trees. Moisture-retentive slightly alkaline soil, although rather more than usually tolerant of drier situations. Moderately hardy, tolerates -15°C (5°F) in winter.
SIZE 1-2m (3-6ft) after one year, then, when established will reach 2-3m (6-10ft) each year.
PROPAGATION Fairly easy from semi-ripe cuttings In late summer, layering or seeds.

" Almost certainly, the 'finest little clematis that Texas ever grew' and one of the few really important North American species to contribute to our gardens. Its varieties are very useful and lovely plants and none is too vigorous. In most of its forms it shares something of the bell-like pendulous flowers of the Asiatic autumn-flowering species, and yet with a quite different colour range in which rich scarlet predominates. I have found it important, nonetheless, to keep the Americans and Asians apart for the red of the former and the yellow of the latter can create a bilious blend. Some of the most effective uses that I have seen for Clematis texensis *have been when it was grown over a low evergreen shrub such as box or yew, in much the same manner as tends to be done*

C. texensis 'Duchess of Albany'

C. texensis 'Princess Diana'

with Tropaeolum speciosum. *The fact that the clematis requires cutting back hard each year makes this a very effective planting idea. It should be said that the species has a reputation for being somewhat tender, but my experience has been that this is rather overstated although some compost mulch around the crown in winter will be beneficial. "*

Clematis pitcheri, from the southern United States, is rather more vigorous but more tender than *C. texensis* and arrestingly lovely. The flowers are almost pitcher-shaped, deep purple within and bluish-purple on the outside but produced rather sparingly.

Clematis viorna (vase vine), from the eastern United States, should be seen more often, but really for its curiosity value more than for any outright beauty. Its flowers, too, are more or less pitcher-shaped and variable in colour from orange-brown to red-purple with cream tips. It will reach about 3m (10ft) and, like the previous species, is somewhat more tender than *C. texensis*.

Clematis crispa (blue jasmine or curlflower), from the south-eastern United States, is a dainty little thing, about 2m (6ft) tall and with nodding, bell-like bluish-purple flowers with curled, almost white edges. It would look delightful in a small, warm but sheltered corner.

Clematis japonica, a northern Asian interloper into the *C. texensis* group, is an oddity but I'm rather fond of it. It would be hard to describe it as pretty but its deep purple-brown, nodding flowers are hairy on the outside and it will certainly turn heads and prompt questions.

* **RED OR PINK, BELL- OR TULIP-LIKE FLOWERS**
* **NOT VERY VIGOROUS**
* **MODERATELY HARDY**

37

Clematis flammula Fragrant Clematis
(GROUP 3)

66 *Many clematis are scented but this one, with its rich, hawthorn-like perfume, probably deserves the epithet 'fragrant' more than most. It's a southern European and Middle Eastern relative of the familiar* Clematis vitalba *or old man's beard of British hedgerows, and is yet another plant whose relative scarcity in gardens just astonishes me. I suppose, ultimately, the problem must be that gardeners prefer big flowers to its masses of small, milk-white blossoms, yet scrambling through a dark leaved*

OTHER SPECIES

Clematis terniflora (also called *C. maximowicziana*) is a superb and vigorous Asian plant with large leaves and white, perfumed flowers that will reach 6m (20ft) on a warm sheltered wall in mild areas. *Clematis potaninii* (also called *C. fargesii*), from China, is also vigorous and has white flowers but of a distinctive satin-like texture. It is fully hardy in mild areas although sadly never seems to flower very prolifically.

evergreen shrub (I have it growing through a holly), it is a real delight. It is very hardy and fairly vigorous, ultimately reaching about 5m (16ft). 99

Clematis flammula

Clematis campaniflora
(GROUP 3)

Clematis campaniflora

66 *Although closely related to* Clematis viticella, *this exquisite Portuguese species seems more at home in a cooler climate with its mass of tiny, nodding bell-like flowers in the palest lilac-blue. It too is ideally grown through large shrubs or trees, when its small leaves can become almost invisible with the result that the pale flowers appear as if suspended in space like fairy lights.* 99

CLEMATIS Evergreen species

Clematis armandii
(GROUP 1)

SITE AND SOIL Preferably sheltered, on a warm sunny wall. Moisture-retentive slightly alkaline soil. Fairly hardy, tolerates between -5 and -10°C (23-14°F) in winter.
SIZE 1-2m (3-6ft) after one year, 4-5m (13-16ft) ultimately.
PROPAGATION Difficult from cuttings, easiest by layering; plants raised from seed are very variable.

'Apple Blossom' has pink buds that open to yield the usual white flowers, 'Snowdrift' is a slight improvement on the true species with its large, attractively bronzed leaves and very good fragrance.

Clematis armandii **'Snowdrift'**

❝ *It is one of the great sadnesses of temperate gardening that most evergreen clematis are too tender to be grown successfully outdoors in any other than the mildest areas. The one significant exception is* Clematis armandii *from China, but I am never really sure just how hardy it is for I have seen it fail in relatively mild gardens, and yet know one wind-swept spot in eastern England where it is as rampant as anyone could wish. Where it does succeed, it is a pleasure to behold with its thick and glossy leaves and, in spring, a mass of large white flowers, usually with five 'petals' and exuding a rich sweet perfume. It is a plant that grows best when unconfined, in the sense that it is allowed room to ramble without the need for pruning and is also not too tightly or closely trained.* ❞

✻ **VERY FRAGRANT WHITE FLOWERS**
✻ **SOME YEAR-ROUND APPEAL**
✻ **GOOD FOR A SHELTERED SPOT**

Clematis armandii **'Apple Blossom'**

Clematis cirrhosa
(GROUP 1)

SITE AND SOIL Sheltered, on a warm sunny wall. Moisture-retentive slightly alkaline soil. Barely hardy, tolerates -5°C (23°F) in winter.
SIZE 1-2m (3-6ft) after one year, 4-5m (13-16ft) ultimately but only in very favourable areas.
PROPAGATION Can be difficult from cuttings, easiest by layering.

" The Chelsea Flower Show in London is always full of horticultural delights and it takes a good deal to stop the crowds and turn the heads. In recent seasons, however, the varieties of this evergreen Mediterranean species have achieved precisely that. The special appeal has lain with the spotted flowers, an uncharacteristic feature among those types of clematis with which most gardeners will be familiar. It is unusual too in its flowering period, the large, bell-shaped, usually cream (and sometimes reddish-spotted) flowers appearing from late autumn to spring (sometimes with a few in summer), depending on variety. Although a wild and unkempt scrambler in the wild, Clematis cirrhosa is much less vigorous in cultivation even in the mild areas where it is most successful. "

* **UNUSUALLY FRECKLED FLOWERS**
* **SOME YEAR-ROUND APPEAL**
* **GOOD FOR A SHELTERED SPOT**

Clematis cirrhosa

RECOMMENDED VARIETIES
var. *balearica* (off-white flowers with small reddish specks, attractive leaves, more deeply dissected than those of the true species and probably a little hardier), 'Freckles' (slightly larger flowers than var. *balearica* and with a mass of reddish-purple, rather than red-brown, spots), 'Wisley Cream' (close to the true species, cream flowers, no spots).

Clematis napaulensis
(GROUP 1)

" This really is a plant only for the most sheltered and warm wall in a mild area and I have to confess that it really is a greenhouse species and also not truly an evergreen, but I am including it because it has always appealed to my botanical mind for its sheer cussedness. It is the only plant I know that can be grown outdoors in temperate climates and which loses its leaves in the summer. The foliage is rather delicate in appearance, not the thick tough leaves of the true evergreen types while the small, nodding cream coloured winter flowers are borne in most attractive clusters. Its real value lies in its flowering period; but if only it was a little tougher. "

Clematis armandii **and camellia**

Dregea sinensis (syn. *Wattakaka sinensis*)

SITE AND SOIL Warm, sunny but not hot position with shelter. Requires well prepared and rich, moisture-retentive loam. Barely hardy, tolerates -5°C (23°F) in winter.
SIZE 1m (3ft) after two years, up to 3m (10ft) eventually in favourable conditions.
PROPAGATION Fairly easy, by layering or cuttings.

> *I had always known and thought of this beautiful twining Chinese species solely as a conservatory plant until I saw one growing in a warm sheltered garden in southern England. It had flourished there for many years and this convinces me that many more gardeners with comparable conditions should try it. It is deciduous with more or less rounded hanging inflorescences of small trumpet-shaped fragrant summer flowers – reminiscent of* Hoya *(to which it is related) but without the evident waxiness. The flowers are white or creamy with tiny reddish streaks.*

Dregea sinensis

CARE

Use horizontal support wires against a warm sunny wall. Even in mild areas, give protection to young plants in their first winter. Moist, rich and fertile soil with little tendency to dry out is best. Mulch in late autumn and again in spring, preferably with garden compost or leaf mould. Give a balanced general fertilizer in spring.

PROPAGATION

Layer low-growing shoots in late summer or strike semi-ripe cuttings in sand to which a small amount of peat has been added. Enclose in a propagator with bottom heat of about 25°C (77°F).

PRUNING

None should be necessary but winter-damaged shoots should be cut out in spring. Any wayward shoots can be cut away and the plant re-tied at the same time.

PROBLEMS

None, although when grown in conservatories, prone to mealy bugs.

＊ **UNUSUAL AND FRAGRANT FLOWERS**
＊ **NOT VERY VIGOROUS**
＊ **APPEALING TWINING HABIT**

FALLOPIA

Fallopia baldschuanica Russian vine, Mile-a-minute vine

Fallopia baldschuanica

❝ Some years ago, I had occasion to clear a small garden that had all but disappeared beneath this rampant, twining plant from central Asia. Only when the thing had been razed to the ground did I realize that it was in fact being supported by an almost completely moribund laburnum that had vanished from view. It is almost too well known to need describing and although often maligned for its vigour, in practice its masses of white or pale pink flowers, produced in summer, can be most attractive. It is its speed of growth rather than its ultimate size that sets it apart and it, therefore, has its uses where an unsightly object must be covered very quickly. Bear in mind, however, that being deciduous, the cover it offers in winter is much less effective. ❞

CARE

Other than against a natural support, some wires will be required in the first stages of growth but thereafter, the plant will become entangled with itself and more or less self-supporting. Almost any type of soil will be suitable, other than those very dry and impoverished. Mulch in late autumn in the first year. No feeding is necessary unless to aid initial establishment.

PROPAGATION

Layer low-growing shoots in late summer or strike semi-ripe cuttings in a 50:50 sand and peat mixture in a cold frame.

PRUNING

None necessary, but can be cut back as hard as required in early spring without fear of damage.

PROBLEMS

None.

✳ **FOAMY MASSES OF SUMMER BLOSSOM**

✳ **VERY FAST GROWING**

✳ **TOLERANT OF ALMOST ALL SITES**

Ficus pumila Creeping fig, Climbing fig

SITE AND SOIL In a protected situation with shelter; preferably a warm, sunny aspect. Best in a moist, organic but not waterlogged soil. Barely hardy, tolerates no lower than -5°C (23°F) in winter and must not be exposed to wind.
SIZE 1m (3ft) after two or three years, up to 4-5m (13-16ft) eventually in favourable situations.
PROPAGATION Fairly easy, from layering or semi-ripe cuttings.

❝ Ficus, *with over 800 species, is not only a very large genus, it is also a very odd one. It includes, of course, the edible fig and also two popular indoor foliage plants, the weeping fig and the rubber plant, neither of which bears much of a resemblance to the other. But it also includes a much less well known climber,* Ficus pumila, *from eastern Asia, that bears little resemblance to either of them. I think it both delightful and very effective; I know one very old walled kitchen garden in Devon where it covers a considerable expanse of the brickwork. It is evergreen, self-clinging by means of tiny aerial roots and exists in two distinct states. The juvenile phase has small, heart-shaped leaves; the adult phase has larger leaves and bears the flowers and fruit. Outdoors, in a sheltered spot in a cool temperate climate, it normally remains in the former condition; in a warm conservatory, the adult phase will also develop.* ❞

Ficus pumila

CARE
Best grown against a fairly flat but very sheltered surface such as a brick wall or tree trunk. It may need lightly tying-in until established. Mulch in late autumn and again in spring with leaf mould or garden compost. Give a balanced general fertilizer in spring.

PROPAGATION
Layer in autumn or take semi-ripe cuttings of the current year's shoots in late summer and strike them in a 50:50 mixture of sand and peat in a

Ficus pumila 'Minima'

shaded frame or propagator, using bottom heat of about 22°C (72°F).

PRUNING
None necessary, but trim back shoots in spring to encourage a better branching habit and more uniform coverage of the support.

PROBLEMS
None.
✳ **CLOSELY CLINGING FRESH GREEN HABIT**
✳ **EVERGREEN**
✳ **FAIRLY TENDER**

HEDERA

Ivies are indispensible, being among the very few evergreen, self-clinging and hardy climbers. But the genus *Hedera* to which they belong includes around 10 or 11 species and a large number of varieties, varying greatly in vigour and in leaf size. It is most important, therefore, to choose carefully for any given situation. Ivies cling very tightly by means of aerial roots with adhesive pads and gardeners are often concerned about the damage that they may cause to the structure on which they are growing, but on sound brick or stonework and mortar, no harm will ensue.

On old, crumbly bricks and mortar, ivies can, however, be destructive. They will also (like many other climbers) lift roof tiles or slates and like other self-clinging species, cause marks on paintwork. They should not be allowed to climb on small, young trees and, while they will not cause direct harm to mature trees (and indeed form a valuable sanctuary for wildlife), a massive growth of ivy in the crown can cause a shallowly rooted tree to become unstable and prone to being blown down in gales.

Ivies occur in juvenile and adult forms, the latter, with different and often less attractively shaped leaves, bears flowers and fruit. The transition from juvenile to adult state often takes place when the top of the wall or other support has been reached, but in other instances the stimulus is obscure and some varieties appear to be almost permanently juvenile. A few varieties are unexpectedly not climbers at all, but upright in form and can almost appear like miniature trees.

Hedera helix 'Adam'

Hedera helix
Common ivy, English ivy

SITE AND SOIL In sun, moderate or full shade in most soils. Hardy, tolerates -20°C (-4°F) in winter although paler-leaved forms may be scorched by extreme cold.
SIZE Very variable, from 1m (3ft) (low vigour) to 15m (50ft) (vigorous) in 10 years.
PROPAGATION Fairly easy, from semi-ripe cuttings or layering.

CARE

Will grow on almost any surface without additional support but note my comments (pages 8 and 13) regarding old brickwork and trees. When newly planted, ivies may not climb for two or three years while they form a mound of growth, and my experience has been that nothing will induce them to grow vertically until they are ready to do so. Mulch in late autumn and again in spring with well rotted manure or garden compost and give a dressing of a balanced general fertilizer in spring, at least until established.

PROPAGATION

Take semi-ripe cuttings of juvenile shoots in late summer and strike in a 50:50 mixture of sand and peat in a propagator. They should root within six months. As an alternative, layer low-growing branches in winter. Natural layers are often found and make the most convenient method of propagation. It is seldom worth propagating ivies from seed, for most named varieties do not come true.

> " This is easily the commonest European species and the one that has given rise to the numerous references to ivy in literature, poetry and song. 'As creeping ivy clings to wood or stone and hides the ruin that it feeds upon', wrote Cowper with a fair degree of horticultural perception. I am still dismayed, however, by the number of gardeners who think only of the true wild species and dismiss it as boring, dull and little more than a creeping woody weed. Among its nearly 400 varieties is surely a plant for every climbing situation. They vary in leaf colour, variegation, size, waviness of the edges, number and shape of lobes, branching habit, vigour and other features. "

Hedera helix **'Goldchild'**

PRUNING

None really necessary when grown in semi-wild situations, but ivies will tolerate being cut back when they threaten to outgrow their situation. This is best performed in spring and, on vigorous plants, may be done with powered hedge trimmers, although ivies regenerate rather slowly when cut back into wood older than about four or five years.

PROBLEMS

None really serious, although leaf spots and blotches caused by fungal attack can be disfiguring. Aphids, red spider mites and scale insects are occasionally troublesome.

✳ **SELF-CLINGING HABIT**
✳ **WILL GROW ALMOST ANYWHERE**
✳ **HUGE VARIETY IN LEAF FORM**

Hedera helix **'Orio di Bogliasco'**

Hedera helix **'Green Ripple'**

RECOMMENDED VARIETIES

'Adam' (small, silver-variegated leaves, low vigour), 'Buttercup' (young leaves golden-yellow, moderate vigour), 'Caecilia' (cream leaves with frilled green edges, low vigour), 'Duckfoot' (small green leaves with rounded lobes, low vigour), 'Eva' (small cream and green leaves, low vigour), 'Glacier' (green and silver-grey leaves, low vigour), 'Goldchild' (golden leaves, low vigour), 'Green Ripple' (irregularly lobed, dark green leaves, moderate vigour), 'Ivalace' (small, dark green leaves with upturned edges, low vigour), 'Little Diamond' (silver-variegated leaves, low vigour), 'Luzii' (small, gold and green-marbled leaves, low vigour), 'Oro di Bogliasco', also called 'Goldheart' (green leaves with golden central blotch, vigorous), 'Parsley Crested' (bright green leaves with wavy margin, moderate vigour), 'Saggitifolia' (slender green, five-lobed leaves, vigorous), 'Très Coupé' (very small green, five-lobed leaves, low vigour).

SIMILAR SPECIES

Hedera hibernica (Irish Ivy) from the western coasts of Europe and the Iberian peninsula is very similar and sometimes considered a variety, but is stronger growing and larger leaved than *H. helix*. The true species is a good garden plant but other notable varieties are 'Deltoidea' (triangular green leaves with heart-shaped overlapping bases), 'Hamilton' (paler green leaves), 'Sulphurea' (green-grey leaves with yellow blotches and edges).

Hedera helix **'Duckfoot'**

Hedera hibernica **'Sulphurea'**

Hedera colchica
Persian Ivy

SITE AND SOIL In sun or moderate shade in most soils, including dry sites. Moderately hardy, tolerates -15°C (5°F) in winter although will be scorched by very cold winds.
SIZE 2m (6ft) after two years, up to 8m (25ft) eventually.
PROPAGATION Fairly easy, from semi-ripe cuttings or layering.

❝ Some of the most spectacular and beautiful ivies that you will ever see belong to this species which, despite its name, originates in the Caucasus and is therefore hardier than you might otherwise imagine. The most obvious difference from the common ivy is in the size of the leaves which can be up to 25cm (10in) across in some varieties. But its leaf size is matched by its vigour and it really is no plant for a confined space. ❞

CARE

Not really at its best when grown against too tall a support. It achieves its most useful purpose when allowed to grow over a large tree stump or when enveloping a low wall. It may need tying-in lightly until established. Mulch in late autumn and again in spring with leaf mould or garden compost. Give a balanced general fertilizer in spring, at least until well established.

PROPAGATION

Take semi-ripe cuttings of juvenile shoots in late summer and strike

H. colchica 'Dentata Variegata'

them in a 50:50 mixture of sand and peat in a shaded frame or propagator. They should root within six months but it is important to trim off most of the leaves from cuttings and also to cut down those remaining by at least half. Alternatively, layer low-growing branches in winter. Natural layers are often found and make the most convenient method of propagation. It is not worth propagating from seed for the named varieties do not come true.

PRUNING

None really necessary when grown in semi-wild situations, but will tolerate being cut back when they threaten to outgrow their situation. This is best done in spring but, unlike the small leaved species, *Hedera colchica* will look something of a mess if cut with powered trimmers. Try to

Hedera colchica 'Sulphur Heart'

RECOMMENDED VARIETIES

'Dentata' (green leaves with small teeth), 'Dentata Variegata' (green leaves with green-grey patches and whitish margins), 'Sulphur Heart', also called 'Paddy's Pride', (superb, with pale green leaves and paler green and yellow blotches in the centre).

avoid cutting into wood older than about four or five years.

PROBLEMS

None really serious, although leaf spots and blotches caused by fungal attack can be disfiguring. Aphids, red spider mites and scale insects are occasionally troublesome.

✳ **SELF-CLINGING HABIT**
✳ **SPECTACULARLY LARGE LEAVES**
✳ **TOLERANT OF DRY CONDITIONS**

Hedera canariensis (syn. *H. algeriensis*) Algerian Ivy

❝ *The most vigorous ivy that I have ever grown was a variety of* Hedera canariensis, *a similar species to* H. colchica. *I had planted it to cover an old low brick wall but it made a valiant attempt to take over my entire kitchen garden too, before I had to curtail its ambitions. Although it extended a long way, it was the ground-covering effect of its large shiny leaves that created the biggest problems so, while it is a beautiful plant, don't say that you haven't been warned.* **❞**

H. canariensis 'Marginomaculata'

Hedera azorica 'Pico'

Hedera nepalensis

RECOMMENDED VARIETIES

Hedera canariensis 'Gloire de Marengo' (dark green leaves with silver-grey surround and white margins), 'Marginomaculata' (green and cream spotted and marbled leaves), 'Montgomery' (smaller, dark green leaves).

OTHER IVIES

Hedera azorica is a more upright-growing plant having bright green leaves with the stems, leaf stalks and leaf undersides bearing a reddish felt. Fairly hardy, tolerates -10°C (14°F) in winter.

Hedera rhombea (Japanese Ivy) has oval, usually unlobed green leaves and a misleadingly fragile appearance. It is more commonly seen in the variety 'Variegata' which has white leaf margins. Moderately hardy, tolerates -15°C (5°F) in winter.

Hedera nepalensis (Himalayan Ivy) has shiny, elongated leaves with occasional small lobes. Most attractive in the adult phase when it bears orange or yellow fruits. Fairly hardy, tolerates -5 to -10°C (23-14°F) in winter.

Hedera rhombea

Holboellia coriacea

SITE AND SOIL Most aspects, tolerant of cool and shady walls. Best in well prepared and rich loam. Fairly hardy, tolerates -10°C (14°F) in winter.
SIZE 2m (6ft) after three years, up to 8m (25ft) eventually.
PROPAGATION Fairly easy, by layering or cuttings.

❝ Considering how scarce are good, evergreen climbers, I am constantly surprised that more gardeners don't grow this very effective, if slightly tender, twining Chinese plant. It has dark green, glossy leaves with three leaflets and, in sunny positions, the bonus of small pendulous flowers – white male and green-white female ones, both flushed with purple. In very warm seasons, sausage-shaped purple fruits may occasionally be produced. If you are prepared to forego the likelihood of blooms however, Holboellia *makes a good plant for a cool and shady wall. ❞*

CARE

Although *Holboellia coriacea* will perfectly well climb small trees, as it does in the wild, in gardens it is best grown against a wall where it will benefit from the shelter. Use horizontal support wires and tie in the plant in the early stages; thereafter, it will climb satisfactorily. Although tolerant of dryness, it grows best in a rich moist soil so mulch in late autumn and again in spring, preferably

SIMILAR SPECIES

Holboellia latifolia, from the Himalayas, is very similar but more tender and vigorous with notably more fragrant flowers.
Sinofranchetia chinensis, from China, is a close relative requiring similar cultivation conditions although it is evergreen and more vigorous, reaching 15m (50ft) in good conditions. The flowers are whitish and insignificant but the large three-lobed leaves are distinctly handsome and the plant can be very effective when covering an old building. Although notionally unisexual, this appears to be only partially correct for the grapelike fruits sometimes occur on female plants without the presence of a male pollinator.
Stauntonia hexaphylla, from Japan and Korea, is another evergreen, similar to the preceding species but less hardy, tolerating about -5°C (23°F), and with rather more attractive purplish flowers. Like *Sinofranchetia*, it too is only supposedly unisexual although the fruits really require regularly hot summers to be produced reliably. Because of the scarcity of good evergreen climbers, it is well worth considering for mild gardens.

with garden compost or leaf mould. Give a balanced general fertilizer in spring, at least until well established.

PROPAGATION

Layer low-growing shoots in late autumn or winter. Alternatively, take semi-ripe cuttings of the current year's shoots in late summer and strike them in a 50:50 mixture of

Holboellia coriacea

sand and peat in a shaded frame or propagator, using bottom heat of about 23°C (73°F) if conditions are cool. Seed is hardly ever set in temperate gardens but, if available, it should be sown in autumn, in sand, in clay pans and left outside overwinter. It should then germinate in spring.

PRUNING

None necessary if growing in semi-natural situations, but against a wall, it may need to be pruned in spring to restrict it to the allotted space.

PROBLEMS

None.

✱ **EVERGREEN HABIT**
✱ **UNUSUAL LEAF FORM FOR A HARDY EVERGREEN**
✱ **FAIRLY HARDY**

Humulus lupulus
Common hop

SITE AND SOIL Warm, sunny position, preferably with shelter from winds. Requires well prepared and rich, moisture-retentive loam. Moderately hardy, tolerates -15°C (5°F) in winter.
SIZE Once established, 7m (23ft) within a season.
PROPAGATION Easy, by cuttings.

❝ *Really good hardy herbaceous climbers can almost be counted on the fingers of one hand and there will always be room for this one, the species whose fruiting head or 'cone' is used in brewing to flavour beer. It has large, somewhat vine-like leaves with coarse teeth and markedly rough twining stems. Although it dies down totally above soil level in winter, the growth during the summer is considerable and this isn't a plant for restricted space. Bear in mind, too, that it offers no screening cover for several months of the year. Despite these shortcomings, however, the hop, especially in its golden-leaved variety, is a splendid plant for a pergola, archway, an old hedge or large pillar.* ❞

CARE
Never at its best when grown against a wall; this plant will need some tying-in on most types of support, as the mass of top growth tends to be blown around in strong winds.

Humulus lupulus '**Aureus**'

Plant in rich, well prepared, moisture-retentive soil, and mulch in late autumn and again in spring, with well rotted manure or garden compost. Give a balanced rose or other flowering-shrub fertilizer in spring.

PROPAGATION
Take leaf-bud cuttings in early summer or semi-ripe stem cuttings slightly later and strike them in a 50:50 peat and sand mixture in a propagator using a bottom heat of 20-22°C (68-72°F) if conditions are cool. Plants raised from seed are very variable and of little value.

PRUNING
None necessary during the growing season but cut back all top growth to about 30cm (12in) above the base in late autumn and then back to soil level in spring.

RECOMMENDED VARIETIES
The true species has green leaves and attractive yellow-brown 'cones'. Selected commercial varieties such as 'Fuggle' may sometimes be available but 'Aureus', with golden leaves, is the most attractive garden plant. *Humulus japonicus*, a more vigorous species with light green leaves, is occasionally offered but is less attractive and, being less hardy, is better grown as an annual.

PROBLEMS
None.
* **VERY VIGOROUS ANNUAL GROWTH**
* **LUSH GOLDEN FOLIAGE**
* **UNUSUAL AND STRIKING 'CONES'**

Every gardener knows the hydrangea, either as the red and pink mopheads that are the standbys of seaside shrubberies or as one of several other, even lovelier and more delicately flowered woodland species. Many will also be familiar with the deciduous oriental climbing species, *Hydrangea anomala* ssp. *petiolaris* but very few indeed will know of the closely related deciduous genus *Schizophragma* and the evergreen *Pileostegia* from the Far East, *Decumaria* from the United States or of a true evergreen climbing *Hydrangea* from South America. A characteristic feature of both *Hydrangea* and *Schizophragma* is the presence, with the usual fertile flowers, of a greater or lesser number of rather large sterile flowers which give these plants much of their ornamental appeal.

Hydrangea anomala ssp. *petiolaris*
Climbing hydrangea

SITE AND SOIL Any aspect, including cool shady walls. Most soils but best in rich, moisture-retentive loam. Moderately hardy, tolerates -15°C (5°F) in winter.
SIZE 3m (10ft) after three years, up to 20m (60ft) eventually.
PROPAGATION Fairly easy, by cuttings.

  66 *I remember well the first time that I planted a climbing hydrangea. I had initially been entranced by its rich, peeling coppery stems in winter and was later captivated by its rounded lush green leaves and its billowing white summer flowers. I was impressed too by its tightly self-clinging aerial roots. Only later, however, did I appreciate its vigour as it almost unstoppably covered a very large wall. Yes, this is a very fine climber, given adequate room, although it must be said that if you expect something akin to a shrubby hydrangea but vertical, you may be disappointed, for the flowers are never as large or showy in the climbing species.* 99

Hydrangea anomala ssp. *petiolaris*

CARE

Climbing hydrangeas often take a few years to begin to climb. While I am unsure if anything will really persuade them until they are ready, they certainly look tidier if the young stems are tied to wall nails or to horizontal wires fitted more or less flat against the wall. This initial tying-in is also useful as it enables the shoots to be arranged in a fan pattern and so ensure that, ultimately, the surface is covered more or less uniformly. They can also be allowed to grow as they do naturally up trees, but this should only be done if the tree really is very large and very robust. They are cer-

SIMILAR SPECIES

Hydrangea anomala, from China and the Himalayas, is similar but less vigorous and with fewer of the showy sterile flowers.
Schizophragma hydrangeoides, from Japan and Korea, is essentially similar to the true hydrangeas when not in flower. Its major difference is that each branch of the inflorescence bears a single, elongated white sepal (flushed pinkish in the variety 'Roseum').
Schizophragma integrifolium, from China, is to my mind the most attractive of the group for both leaves and inflorescences are larger than in the preceding species. In general, schizophragmas have the slight drawback of being rather slower to establish than *Hydrangea anomala* ssp. *petiolaris* but are equally hardy though slightly less vigorous, ultimately reaching perhaps 10m (33ft) rather than 20m (60ft).

tainly not plants to train against trellis or wires.

Good rich soil is essential and this must not be allowed to dry out so mulch in late autumn and again in spring, preferably with compost or, best of all, with leaf mould. Give a balanced general fertilizer in spring, at least until well established.

Pileostegia viburnoides

Schizophragma integrifolium

PROPAGATION

Best by semi-hardwood cuttings in late summer in a 50:50 sand and peat mixture with bottom heat of 22°C (72°F). Softwood cuttings in spring may also be successful. Plants raised from seed are likely to be variable.

PRUNING

None necessary, but if outgrowing its allotted space, may be cut back as hard as necessary in spring.

PROBLEMS

None.

- **CLUSTERS OF WHITE FLOWERS**
- **VIGOROUS AND SELF-CLINGING**
- **ATTRACTIVE WINTER BARK**

Hydrangea serratifolia

“ I have struggled with this plant over many years but have been forced to conclude that my garden is just too cold. I count this a great pity for there are so few really attractive self-clinging evergreen climbers. The leaves are elongated and very glossy and the small white summer flowers no cause for great excitement but a useful bonus. It has two significant characteristics: first, and one that I learned the hard way, it is barely hardy, about -5°C (23°F) being all that it can reliably tolerate before its leaves become browned, although in mild or well sheltered gardens it will certainly flourish; second, it is phenomenally vigorous and in its native Chilean forests will reach 40m (130ft). It is ideally planted to grow up very large and robust trees, although it would equally well envelop unsightly large walls and buildings. ”

SIMILAR SPECIES

Hydrangea seemannii, from Mexico, is being encountered more regularly in nursery catalogues. It differs in its rather larger, prettier and slightly pinkish flowers but seems to be less vigorous.

Pileostegia viburnoides, from India and China, is an evergreen version of *Schizophragma* with white flowers in late summer although it is perhaps slightly more tender and rather less vigorous, reaching about 5-6m (16-20ft). Being evergreen and self-clinging, however, it has similiar value to the evergreen hydrangeas.

Decumaria barbara

“ Considering that this North American plant has been cultivated in Britain since the late eighteenth century, it is remarkably little known, even in sheltered gardens. It will ultimately reach about 9m (30ft). Whereas the related genera derive much of their appeal through their mixture of fertile and sterile flowers, the white summer blossom of Decumaria *is composed entirely of small fragrant fertile flowers, all with obvious stamens. It differs too in being semi-evergreen and more tender, tolerating no less than -10°C (14°F). ”*

Decumaria barbara

SIMILAR SPECIES

Decumaria sinensis, from China, the only other species, has similar flowers but is fully evergreen, less vigorous, reaching about 5m (16ft) and less hardy, tolerating about -5°C (23°F).

The genus *Jasminum* is a large one in the olive family and embraces around 200 evergreen and deciduous species. In temperate gardens, however, only a handful are cultivated regularly. One is a very popular shrub, the yellow flowered winter jasmine, *Jasminum nudiflorum*, while the others are exquisite climbers. They are, moreover, plants that really straddle the boundary between the true shrub and climber categories, the so-called climbers really being only just able to support themselves.

Jasminum officinale
Common Jasmine, Summer Jasmine

❝ There can be no finer evocation of the glory of summer in an English garden than this exquisitely perfumed white flowered climber. Although it originated in central Asia, it was introduced to the West as early as the middle of the sixteenth century and it is hard to imagine that we ever gardened without it. Its mass of small, tubular flowers in little clusters set against a ferny green foliage would be attractive enough, but it is that light sweet fragrance that is its ultimate glory. Although deciduous, this jasmine retains an out of season appeal in its pliable greenish stems, and it is one of the very few climbers that I feel looks effective on a house wall even when in its almost inevitable, slightly unkempt, tangle. ❞

RECOMMENDED VARIETIES

'Argenteovariegatum' is also called 'Variegatum' (white-variegated leaves), 'Aureum' (leaves with golden-yellow blotches, less hardy), f. *affine* is also called 'Grandiflorum' (larger, pink tinged flowers).

SITE AND SOIL A warm, sunny wall, preferably with a good, fairly rich, moisture-retentive loam. In cold areas, grow in a sheltered, sunny position. Moderately hardy, tolerates -10 to -15°C (14-5°F) in winter.

SIZE 2m (6ft) after three years, up to 10m (30ft) or more eventually if unpruned.

PROPAGATION Easy, especially by layering.

CARE

Although *Jasminum officinale* will become pretty well self-supporting if planted free-standing and close pruned, it is seen best (and its fragrance most appreciated) against a house wall, tied loosely to horizontal support wires. It is moderately tolerant of soil dryness and quite intolerant of waterlogging. Mulch in late autumn and again in spring, preferably with garden compost or leaf mould. Give a balanced rose or other flowering shrub fertilizer in spring.

Jasminum officinale

PROPAGATION

Layer low-growing shoots in late autumn or winter; this is much the simplest method of propagation and

Jasminum x stephanense

OTHER SPECIES

Jasminum beesianum, from China, is very unusual in its red flowers which are followed by a mass of black fruits that tend to be ignored by birds and will persist until well into the winter.

Jasminum x stephanense is an artificial hybrid between *J. officinale* and *J. beesianum* although the same cross does occur in the wild. The flowers are pink. Although fast to establish, it will ultimately reach only about 5m (16ft).

Jasminum mesnyi (Primrose Jasmine) is a yellow bloomed summer-flowering evergreen species, beautiful but barely hardy, tolerating no less than about -3°C (26°F) in winter.

Jasminum polyanthum is a semi-evergreen species with white, pink flushed flowers, most familiar as the pot plant usually called 'indoor jasmine'. It too is barely hardy, tolerating no less than about -5°C (23°F).

natural layers are commonly found. Semi-ripe cuttings may be taken in late summer and struck in a 50:50 peat and sand mixture in a propagator with very gentle or no bottom heat. Seed is not usually set in temperate conditions but, if available, it should be sown in autumn in sand in clay pans and left outside overwinter. It should then germinate in spring.

PRUNING

It is almost impossible to create a tidy plant of a summer jasmine and I simply prune out frost-damaged, over-long and overcrowded stems in spring, re-tying where necessary. Always cut back to the junction with a strong parent stem or to the base of the plants.

PROBLEMS

Some frost damage, often extended by *Botrytis,* may be expected in most localities and aphids may also be troublesome.

✳ **EXQUISITE PERFUME**

✳ **DAINTY, FERN-LIKE FOLIAGE**

✳ **EASY TO GROW IN ALL EXCEPT VERY COLD AREAS**

Jasminum mesnyi

Lapageria rosea
Chilean Bellflower

SITE AND SOIL A warm, sunny and very sheltered wall with a rich, organic, preferably acid loam. Barely hardy, tolerating only -5°C (23°F) in winter.

SIZE 1m (3ft) after two years, up to 5m (16ft) eventually in favourable positions.

PROPAGATION Easy, by layering or seed.

66 *What finer horticultural credibility can a plant have than to be named after that most regal of gardeners, the Empress Josephine (whose maiden name was de la Pagerie), and also to have the added status of being a national flower, in this case of Chile?* Lapageria *is worthy of the honour on both counts, being one of that small group of luscious South American evergreens that have found their way to Europe. The crimson flowers last from mid-summer through to the autumn and are indeed bell-like with thick, fleshy segments, while the foliage is dark green and elegant in its simplicity. There is, of course, a drawback: it isn't very hardy, but for anyone with a sheltered mild garden and appropriate soil, it is a gem.* 99

CARE

Plant against a warm wall and tie in the twining shoots to horizontal wires until it is well established. The soil must be rich, moisture-retentive,

Lapageria rosea

organic and lime-free (preferably slightly acid). Mulch in late autumn and again in spring, best with garden compost, leaf mould or shredded conifer needles. Give a balanced rose or other flowering-shrub fertilizer in spring. In more or less neutral soils, *Lapageria* seems to respond particularly well to an application of sequestered iron in early spring although curiously the plant seldom seems to exhibit the leaf yellowing symptoms often displayed by acid loving species.

PROPAGATION

Layer low-growing shoots in late autumn or winter; this is much the simplest method of propagation and natural layers may sometimes be found. Seed is occasionally offered for sale but should be rejected if dry. It ought to be sold fresh, complete with its jelly-like protective coat. This must then be washed off and

Lapageria rosea **'Albiflora'**

Lapageria rosea **'Nash Court'**

the seeds sown fresh in a sandy, soil-based compost at a temperature of about 20°C (68°F); it should then germinate within about three months. It is however, extremely important that the seed is washed thoroughly to remove the germination inhibitors present in the jelly. I have done this most successfully by standing the seeds overnight in water, shaking them thoroughly in the morning and then throwing away the water. I then add fresh water and repeat the process twice more. Plants raised from seed are variable in vigour but interesting, for a number of colour variants may turn up; the beautiful white flowered form (see above) apparently always comes true from seed.

PRUNING

None necessary, but can be tidied in late spring by cutting wayward or cold-damaged shoots back to a bud, or to the junction with their parent stem. Congested growth should be thinned out in spring.

PROBLEMS

Mealy bugs, scale insects and aphids can cause problems but usually only on conservatory or cold greenhouse plants; the former two pests are rarely troublesome in the open.

✳ **SUPERBLY EXOTIC LOOKING FLOWERS**

✳ **LUSH, EVERGREEN FOLIAGE**

✳ **NOT VERY VIGOROUS**

RECOMMENDED VARIETIES

'Albiflora' (white flowers), 'Flesh Pink' (lustrous silver-pink flowers), 'Nash Court' (dark pink to red flowers).

Rare indeed is the gardener who cannot recognize a honeysuckle, and deprived is the gardener who has never grown one. But in saying this, I do believe that they are not plants for the small, neat, tidy and kempt modern garden; their habit is too straggly to be satisfactorily confined on a house wall. On the side of a rambling country cottage, however, they are as at home as in their natural woodland setting.

The honeysuckle genus, *Lonicera,* includes around 180 species but many are shrubs rather than climbers and many, sadly, too tender for temperate gardens. The climbers are tough, woody twining plants and include both deciduous and evergreen species, all sharing the familiar irregular form of the white, yellow or reddish flowers, and most are richly perfumed. I have divided them loosely into the more or less deciduous species, the more or less evergreen species and the hybrids and have given general notes on their care and cultivation on page 60.

Lonicera periclymenum 'Belgica'

Lonicera implexa

Lonicera caprifolium

Lonicera etrusca 'Superba'

Lonicera sempervirens

Lonicera periclymenum
Common honeysuckle, Woodbine

SITE AND SOIL Generally best in light shade but will tolerate almost all situations and aspects although least effective in very windy places. Gives unsatisfactory results in poor soils, best in rich, deep organic loam. Hardy, tolerates at least -15°C (5°F) in winter.
SIZE 2m (6ft) after two or three years, up to 4-5m (13-16ft) eventually.
PROPAGATION Easy, especially from layers.

✳ **UNUSUALLY SHAPED FRAGRANT FLOWERS**
✳ **WILL GROW ALMOST ANYWHERE**
✳ **VERY TOUGH**

❝ *Honeysuckle is one of the best known and best loved British plants, either in the wild form that garlands the hedgerows ('quite over-canopied with luscious woodbine' as Shakespeare saw it) or its garden varieties. No member of the genus more exemplifies my view that this is a plant for an informal setting. As much as anything this is because, while the varieties as a whole span a considerable flowering period, no one plant will be in bloom for long enough to justify its rather ragged appearance for the rest of the year. But for the person with* both the desire and the room to recreate the appeal of a traditional cottage garden, and willing to let the thing do pretty much as it pleases, Lonicera periclymenum *is indispensible. The sweet fragrance as its flowers are caught by the first warm sunlight of a dewy summer morning is a richness indeed.* ❞

RECOMMENDED VARIETIES
'Belgica' (Early Dutch honeysuckle) produces purple-red flowers fading to reddish-yellow, fragrant, less vigorous, in early summer, 'Graham Thomas' produces large white-yellow flowers in mid-summer to autumn, 'Serotina' (Late Dutch honeysuckle) produces purple-red flowers, yellow within, in late summer to autumn.

Lonicera periclymenum 'Serotina'

Lonicera tragophylla

OTHER SPECIES

For site and soil, size and propagation see *Lonicera periclymenum*.

Lonicera caprifolium (Italian Honeysuckle, Perfoliate Honeysuckle). This related deciduous European species is naturalized in Britain. It has the most exquisitely fragrant yellowish, pink-tinged flowers, below which the first few of the bluish-green leaves are united in pairs. The fruits are appealingly orange coloured and, to my mind, this is probably the best all-round garden honeysuckle. Its only real drawback is its considerable vigour, for it will exceed even the wild form of *L. periclymenum* in size.

Lonicera etrusca (Etruscan Honeysuckle) is a southern European species, semi-evergreen in mild areas and with markedly red-purple young shoots. The flowers are richly fragrant, pale cream at first but later becoming reddish tinged and finally deep yellow. There is a fine variety 'Superba' which is more vigorous and with more intense flower colours. This species is markedly less hardy however, barely tolerating less than -10°C (14°F) in winter.

Lonicera tragophylla. All honeysuckles will excite comment but for me the particular appeal of this deciduous Chinese species is the sheer size of its yellow flowers and indeed the sheer size of the whole thing. The only serious drawback is that it doesn't have any appreciable fragrance but if you have a large outbuilding, a very large pergola or similar structure to cover, then this is the honeysuckle to choose. Fairly hardy, tolerates -10°C (14°F) in winter.

Lonicera sempervirens (Trumpet Honeysuckle), from the southern United States, is on the boundary between being evergreen and deciduous, retaining its leaves in mild areas, losing them in the cold. The flowers are rich red on the outside, yellowish within but lacking scent. This is another vigorous plant, reaching 5m (16ft) or more eventually, but only fairly hardy, tolerating -10°C (14°F) in winter. There is a particularly fine form called *sulphurea* in which the flowers are all yellow.

Lonicera japonica
Japanese Honeysuckle

66 This is the best known and, generally speaking, the most useful of all of the evergreen honeysuckles, being tougher and easier to grow than many. It also exists in a number of rather distinct varieties, each with their own merits. In the true species, the flowers are white with a yellowish flush and not especially visually arresting, but they have a long flowering period from early summer to autumn and are deliciously fragrant. They are followed by shiny black fruits, the foliage is fresh and green and I always feel this plant is seen at its best when it is left, unpruned, to cover some large old tree stump or similar support. 99

RECOMMENDED VARIETIES

'Halliana' is the best variety and also the most well-known, with especially fragrant flowers that turn noticeably yellow as they mature. 'Aureoreticulata' is quite different and less vigorous with smaller leaves on which the midrib and veins are yellow. It flowers less readily, certainly away from protection and is less hardy, really requiring the shelter of a warm wall. The very pretty form *repens* has leaves, stem and flowers markedly flushed with purple.

Lonicera henryi

SIMILAR SPECIES

Lonicera henryi, from China, has rather smaller but neater purplish-red perfumed flowers with a yellow flush and, in good conditions, is possibly even more vigorous than *L. japonica*. It also has a longer flowering period, from mid-summer to autumn.

Lonicera alseuosmoides is, I think, less widely grown than it should be because of its unspellable and unpronounceable name. It is very similar to *L. henryi* but more restrained and with more yellowish flowers.

Lonicera japonica 'Halliana'

Lonicera japonica 'Aureoreticulata'

Lonicera splendida

Lonicera hildebrandiana

OTHER SPECIES

Lonicera implexa (Minorca Honeysuckle), from the Mediterranean, is summer-flowering and rather tender, tolerating no less than -5°C (23°F), but in mild places is well worth a try for its low vigour, reaching only about 2-3m (6-10ft), its leaves which are markedly bluish-green beneath, and its pretty although more or less scentless yellow and pink flowers.

Lonicera splendida, from Spain, although evergreen, is in fact closely related to the common *L. periclymenum*. The abundant and fragrant flowers, borne through the summer, are reddish-purple on the outside and white or yellowish within and altogether this is a lovely species, but for a sheltered spot, being similarly hardy to *L. implexa*.

Lonicera hildebrandiana (Giant Burmese honeysuckle) is metaphorically speaking the mother and father of all honeysuckles, a huge and magnificent plant that is larger in all of its parts than any other species of honeysuckle known to science. Once seen in full glory, it is a sight not easily forgotten, with leaves 12cm (5in) long, cream and orange fragrant flowers up to 15cm (6in) long, and the whole thing capable of reaching 25m (80ft) in length. But yes, of course, it's barely hardy and will only just withstand 0°C (32°F). But for anyone with a big, mild and sheltered garden, it is the honeysuckle to try.

There are four truly beautiful deciduous *Lonicera* hybrids that are of real garden merit. Interestingly, at least one of them occurs naturally in the wild but the origins of two of the others are somewhat obscure. None of this need concern the gardener seeking only a delightful embellishment to a relatively informal garden.

Lonicera x tellmaniana (L. tragophylla x L. sempervirens 'Superba')

SITE AND SOIL Best planted in light shade with the head in sun but will tolerate most situations and aspects. Prefers a rich, deep organic loam. Moderately hardy, tolerates -10 to -15°C (14-5°F) in winter.
SIZE 2m (6ft) after two or three years, up to 6-7m (20-23ft) eventually.
PROPAGATION Fairly easy, from cuttings or layers.

❝ I have no hesitation whatsoever in considering this the best of the hybrids and arguably the best of all garden honeysuckles from a visual standpoint, although regrettably it is scentless. It arose as a deliberate cross in Hungary early this century, and unites the characteristics of one of the best Asian and one of the best American species. It produces its large, rich yellow flowers in early summer. It is a vigorous plant and is ideally suited to the semi-shaded situation at the edge of a woodland. ❞

Lonicera x heckrottii

SIMILAR HYBRIDS

Lonicera x heckrottii (L. x americana x L. sempervirens) is less vigorous than the other hybrids, reaching ultimately about 3m (10ft), and as it barely twines, it is in many ways more of a very lax shrub in need of considerable support than a true climber. Its origin is unknown but the flowers which appear in early summer are undeniably lovely, yellow on the inside and pink on the outside with a marked, although not overpowering, fragrance. 'Gold Flame' is the named variety that will almost invariably be seen, but it seems not to differ from the original cross.

Lonicera x tellmaniana

Lonicera x italica

Lonicera x *brownii* (*L. hirsuta* x *L. sempervirens*)
Scarlet Trumpet Honeysuckle

" Yet another exquisite although, again, sadly not fragrant plant. The cross between the two parent species has been made a number of times and several varieties with slightly different characteristics now exist. They all share the unusual feature of rich scarlet, narrowly trumpet-shaped flowers with orange throats, although it must be admitted that this sometimes disappoints those who believe that a honeysuckle should have at least some yellow in its colouration. "

CARE

In general, honeysuckles should be planted where their vigour and rather untidy habit are afforded free rein: against a mature tree so that they climb into and cascade from the lower branches is ideal, but over a pergola or outbuilding is equally effective. They may need lightly tying-in until established. Planted against a house wall, especially a neat, modern house wall, they rarely look right, the exception possibly being the less vigorous *Lonicera* x *heckrottii* 'Gold Flame'. Mulch in late autumn and again in spring with leaf mould or garden compost. Give a balanced rose or similar flowering-shrub fertilizer in spring, at least until well established.

PROPAGATION

Layer in autumn, take semi-ripe cuttings of the current year's shoots in late summer and strike them in a

Lonicera x *brownii* 'Fuchsioides'

50:50 mixture of sand and peat in a shaded frame or propagator; or strike hardwood cuttings in the open garden in winter. The good named varieties don't come true from seed and this method of propagation is scarcely worth the effort.

PRUNING

No two gardeners really seem to agree on this subject but I think there are essentially two approaches. The plants may be left to form a natural and, admittedly, rather unruly tangle or the oldest third of the shoots should be cut back to soil level each spring. If the latter

approach is adopted, it really needs to be done from the beginning with a new plant, as the individual stems soon begin to twine together to form inseparable ropes.

PROBLEMS

Aphids (a honeysuckle-specific type of blackfly) and mildew are almost always present, particularly if the plant is growing in too hot a place, and the former especially will distort leafy and flowering shoots.

* **PARTICULARLY ATTRACTIVE FLOWER COLOURS**
* **SOME WITH GOOD FRAGRANCE**
* **EASY TO GROW**

RECOMMENDED VARIETIES

'Dropmore Scarlet' is the best known and most recent variety, with particularly well coloured flowers and a long flowering season from mid-summer until well into autumn. 'Fuchsioides' has more orange coloured flowers and a more intermittent flowering period.

SIMILAR SPECIES

Lonicera x *americana*, now often called *L.* x *italica* (*L. caprifolium* x *L. etrusca*), is a cross between two European species and does occur, though rarely, in the wild. As in *L. caprifolium*, the uppermost pair of leaves is united in cup fashion, but it is more floriferous and in summer bears a mass of richly fragrant yellow flowers with a purple flush. It has also inherited the relatively greater hardiness of *L. caprifolium*.

When I use the name Virginia creeper, I think most people will know the plants that I have in mind although strictly the name really applies to only one species of *Parthenocissus*. No matter, for I am sure this is the most useful genus of deciduous foliage climbers that we have and there really are few finer ways to clothe a large wall. I do emphasize 'large', nonetheless, for all of these plants are vigorous and can so easily swamp a small support. They climb by means of tendrils but differ from related plants such as *Ampelopsis* in having small adhesive pads at the tips. Their flowers are generally insignificant although the black, shiny fruits can sometimes be attractive.

Parthenocissus tricuspidata Boston Ivy

SITE AND SOIL Almost any aspect, preferably with a good, fairly rich, moisture-retentive loam although tolerant of most soil conditions. Hardy, tolerates -15 to -20°C (5 to -4°F) in winter.
SIZE 2m (6ft) after three years, up to 9m (30ft) or more eventually if unpruned.
PROPAGATION Easy, by layering or cuttings.

CARE
Until established, there may be difficulty in persuading the plant to climb but tying it up is rarely of any benefit. It is best allowed to form a mound of growth at the base of the wall, from which vertical shoots will sooner or later arise. It is fairly tolerant of soil dryness and also of moderate soil moisture, although it will not thrive in waterlogged conditions. Mulch in late autumn and again in spring, preferably with garden compost or leaf mould. Give a balanced general fertilizer in spring.

PROPAGATION
Layer low-growing shoots in late autumn or winter; this is the simplest method of propagation and natural layers are commonly found. Semi-ripe cuttings may be taken in late summer and struck in a 50:50 peat

❝ *I challenge anyone to show me a brick wall more striking than one covered with this plant in autumn as its fairly large, usually three-lobed leaves turn a fiery crimson. Caught in the low rays of the setting sun, you could be forgiven for reaching for dark glasses. In the winter, it is, of course, much less appealing, simply having a wiry network of bare stems but spring soon comes and with it the fresh colours of unfolding buds. Once established, it is very tightly self-clinging by means of the adhesive suckers on its tendrils. Despite its common name, it originates from China and Japan.* ❞

and sand mixture in a propagator with very gentle or no bottom heat.

PRUNING
None is necessary, although in the early stages, it will be found helpful to pinch out some shoots in order to encourage branching and ensure that the wall is covered uniformly. When established, it should be kept clear of window frames and roof tiles or slates. This is best achieved, not with secateurs which will be blunted, but with an old knife, run along the brickwork twice a year

'Beverley Brook' has reddish-purple summer foliage and more orange autumn colours, 'Green Spring' is rather less vigorous than the true species, 'Lowii' has rather small, neatly three- to seven-lobed leaves, 'Veitchii' (still sometimes called *Ampelopsis tricuspidata* 'Veitchii'), is the best known and most widely available form and has rather small three-lobed red-purple leaves.

Parthenocissus tricuspidata

about 15-20cm (6-8in) away from the required limit of spread.

PROBLEMS
None.
✳ **SUPERB AUTUMN FOLIAGE COLOURS**
✳ **SELF-CLINGING HABIT**
✳ **WILL GROW ALMOST ANYWHERE**

Parthenocissus tricuspidata

Parthenocissus quinquefolia

Parthenocissus henryana

OTHER SPECIES

Parthenocissus henryana If you want the *Parthenocissus* with the largest and most beautiful leaves, then this will be your choice. It is more vigorous than *P. tricuspidata* and also slightly less hardy, being better for a sheltered, shady wall where the exquisite leaf patterning attains its greatest intensity. The foliage colour is best described as dark bronze-green with the veins in contrasting pink and whitish. In autumn it turns an intense orange-red. *Parthenocissus quinquefolia* (Virginia Creeper) If you ask for the real Virginia Creeper, this should be the plant you will be sold. As its name suggests, it has five leaflets to each of the green leaves which turn brilliant red and orange in autumn. It never has quite the splendour of *P. henryana*, however, or quite the close neatness of *P. tricuspidata*. The variety *P. engelmannii* has smaller leaves but equally good autumn colours.

There is just nothing to match the extraordinarily bizarre appearance of a passion flower, at least nothing that will grow outdoors in a temperate climate. They are evergreen twining climbers and those few species that can be grown in gardens in Britain are all South American. Although the information will be familiar to many gardeners, there remain many more who puzzle over the origin of the name so I make no apology for repeating the generally accepted version. Missionary priests in South America saw in the flowers a representation of Christ's Passion and used it to teach the story to native peoples. The ten flower segments or tepals were the apostles (minus Judas and Peter), the corona of filaments was the crown of thorns, the five stamens were Christ's wounds, the three stigmas were the nails, the five-lobed leaf was Christ's hand and the leaf tendrils the lashes of his tormenters. A clever story, whether true or not.

Passiflora caerulea Blue Passion Flower

SITE AND SOIL Sunny aspect with a rich, moisture-retentive loam although tolerant of most soil conditions. Fairly hardy, tolerates -5°C (23°F) or slightly less.
SIZE 2m (6ft) after three years, up to 6m (20ft) or more eventually in mild, favourable areas.
PROPAGATION Fairly easy, by layering or cuttings.

For most gardeners, this is the passion flower for it is the only one that I could reliably recommend for those areas with colder climates. It has the familiar and characteristic flower form with a complex array of colours, among which blue predominates. They have a slight but pleasing fragrance. In good warm summers, orange, egg-shaped fruits are formed but, although edible, they are a poor second to the true edible passion fruit from Passiflora edulis, *the tropical granadilla. No passion flower can be guaranteed to survive outdoors permanently but this one is pretty durable and, even when the top growth is killed back by frost, it will usually shoot again.*

Passiflora caerulea

CARE

Best trained against horizontal wires in a warm sunny corner. It will naturally form an untidy tangle so is more satisfactorily tied in a fan or similar pattern. Best in rich, rather moist but not waterlogged soil. Mulch in late autumn and again in spring, preferably with garden compost or leaf mould. Give a rose or other flowering-shrub fertilizer in spring.

PROPAGATION

Layer low-growing shoots in early autumn or take semi-ripe cuttings in late summer and strike them in a 50:50 peat and sand mixture in a propagator with bottom heat of 25°C (77°F). Seed is often available and easy to germinate but plants raised from seed are very variable and I don't recommend this method.

PRUNING

Cut out dead, damaged or weak shoots in the spring but in mild areas, try to maintain a more or less permanent framework of strong shoots. In colder areas, and where the above ground growth is severely damaged by frost, it may be necessary to cut back more or less to soil level but in all except the very coldest conditions, the plants should shoot again from the base, provided a protective mulch has been applied in autumn.

PROBLEMS

Viruses will distort the foliage and seem to render the plants more prone to frost damage. Aphids and whiteflies may also be troublesome.

❋ **EXQUISITE, EXOTIC LOOKING FLOWERS**

❋ **ATTRACTIVE SCRAMBLING HABIT**

❋ **WILL SURVIVE IN FAIRLY COOL AREAS**

Passiflora racemosa

RECOMMENDED VARIETIES

Always buy a selected strain of the true species and preferably see the plant in flower before you do so. 'Constance Elliott' is a lovely white flowered form.

Passiflora caerulea 'Constance Elliott'

SIMILAR SPECIES

Passiflora x *violacea* (*P. caerulea* x *P. racemosa*) has ravishing red pendulous flowers with white and purple bands, although there are also selected varieties such as 'Eynsford Gem' which are more of a purple-pink. It will tolerate about -5°C (23°F).

Passiflora incarnata (Apricot Vine) should be tried more widely as it is more or less herbaceous and dies back to the base each year but will regrow given mulch protection even when the winter temperature falls as low as -15°C (5°F). The flower colours usually include white, pinks and mauves, and a lovely deep purple flowered variety called 'Incense', derived from this species has become rather popular.

PASSION FLOWERS AS CONSERVATORY PLANTS

Although strictly, I am limiting my coverage in the book to hardy plants, I am prepared to come close to making an exception with passion flowers. For this really is a very large genus, containing over five hundred species and among them are several that make fine conservatory plants for putting outdoors during the summer. For this purpose, they should be grown in large ornamental pots (about 30cm (12in) in diameter is ideal) with a high quality soil-based compost such as John Innes No 3. I always think they look their best in terracotta rather than glazed pots, and seem to grow better too. They should be fed sparingly during the winter but then given liquid fertilizer with a high potash content from early spring onwards; and through the summer while they are outside. Among the species that I would commend especially are the vivid red *Passiflora antioquiensis* and *P. manicata* and the nearest that any passion flower approaches to yellow, *P. lutea*.

Passiflora incarnata

Periploca graeca
Silk Vine

SITE AND SOIL Almost any aspect, but flowers best in full sun and in a good, fairly rich, moisture-retentive loam although tolerant of most soil conditions. Fairly hardy, tolerates -10°C (14°F) in winter.
SIZE 2m (6ft) after three years, up to 9m (30ft) or more eventually if unpruned.
PROPAGATION Fairly easy by layering.

" *I first saw* Periploca graeca *growing over a large pergola in a rather fine garden in the south of England and decided, there and then, that I wanted one. In the best gardening tradition, I was given a few cuttings which I struck with some difficulty, for like many plants in the family Asclepiadaceae, they exuded a milky sap which seems to inhibit rooting. But I do now have my silk vine and am delighted to see it appearing more frequently in nursery catalogues. I would be less than honest in calling it a stunningly beautiful species but it is a useful, vigorous and unusual deciduous twining climber from south-east Europe and western Asia with medium-sized yellowish-green flowers with purple-brown insides and a rather peculiar smell.* "

Periploca graeca

CARE

As the habit is slightly straggly, it is best trained against a fairly informal support such as a pergola, archway or old tree. In my experience, it begins to climb very quickly after planting. It is tolerant of a wide range of soil conditions including moderate dryness but it will always be at its best in full sun. Mulch in late autumn and again in spring, preferably with garden compost or leaf mould. Give a balanced rose or other potash-rich fertilizer in spring.

PROPAGATION

Layer low-growing shoots in late autumn or winter; this is much the simplest method of propagation. Semi-ripe cuttings may be taken in late summer and struck with difficulty in a 50:50 peat and sand mixture in a propagator with very gentle or no bottom heat.

PRUNING

None is necessary, although it may be cut back as hard as necessary in spring and will rejuvenate.

PROBLEMS

None.

✳ **UNUSUAL FLOWERS**
✳ **FAIRLY VIGOROUS**
✳ **WILL GROW IN MOST SOILS**

SCHISANDRA

Schisandra rubriflora

SITE AND SOIL Almost any aspect but must have a rich, moisture-retentive loam. Fairly hardy, tolerates -10°C (14°F) in winter.
SIZE 2m (6ft) after three years, up to 6m (20ft) or more eventually if unpruned.
PROPAGATION Fairly easy, by layering.

❝ This is an undeniably striking deciduous twining climber from central China and adjoining areas of Asia. At least, it is undeniably striking when it is bearing its pendulous reddish-pink flowers in almost cherry-like clusters and even more so with its spikes of small round red fruits that hang down like Christmas decorations. Unfortunately, it is a unisexual species and so both male and female individuals will be needed for fruit production. But it is hardy enough and easy to grow so, once again, I find myself wondering why it isn't grown more widely, for a considerable number of nurseries do stock it. ❞

Schisandra rubriflora (female)

Schisandra rubriflora (male)

CARE

Like *Periploca*, it has a somewhat straggly habit, and it too is best grown against a fairly informal support such as a pergola, archway or old tree, although it can be trained on horizontal wires against a tall wall. Two individuals of opposite sex should be planted about 1m (3ft) apart and allowed to interwine once established. They must have a deep, rich and moist soil but are tolerant of shade. Mulch in late autumn and again in spring, preferably with garden compost or leaf mould. Give a balanced rose or other potash-rich fertilizer in spring.

PROPAGATION

Layer low-growing shoots in late autumn or winter; this is the only reliable method of obtaining plants of known sex, for although seed is sometimes available, it will be a long time before the sex of the seedlings becomes apparent.

PRUNING

None is necessary, although it may be cut back in spring to remove unwanted shoots and branches.

PROBLEMS

None.

* **STRIKING RED FRUITS**
* **FAIRLY VIGOROUS**
* **USEFUL FOR SHADE**

Senecio scandens

SITE AND SOIL Almost any aspect, but always flowers best in full sun and in a moisture-retentive loam although tolerant of some soil dryness. Fairly hardy, tolerates -5 to -10°C (23-14°F) in winter.
SIZE 2m (6ft) after three years, up to 5-6m (16-20ft) eventually.
PROPAGATION Fairly easy, by cuttings.

66 I have often mentioned the rarity and value of climbing members of the family Asteraceae and this is another, a real oriental climbing daisy, easy to cultivate, durable and very pretty with its yellow clustered flowers in late summer. It has the typical and characteristic downy grey-green foliage of the shrubby senecios that we know from the mixed border. But unlike many of its relatives, it still retains the name Senecio *when others have fled to* Brachyglottis. 99

CARE

Like most shrubby senecios, this is not a particularly tidy plant and is better suited to a semi-wild, rather than an unashamedly artificial situation. The prettiest examples are usually those allowed to scramble over hedges or low fences. It is tolerant of a wide range of soil conditions including free-draining dry sites but requires full sun for the best flowering. Mulch in late autumn and again in spring, preferably with garden compost or leaf mould. Give a balanced rose or other potash-rich fertilizer in spring.

Senecio scandens

PROPAGATION

Take semi-ripe cuttings in late summer, removing most of the woolly leaves which will trap moisture. Strike them in a sandy soil-based compost in a frame or propagator, supplying bottom of heat of 22-25°C (72-77°F) but with plenty of ventilation. May also be raised from seed sown in a soil-based compost in spring at similar temperatures.

PRUNING

None is necessary, but it is likely to be damaged in cold winters and may then be cut back hard in spring and will rejuvenate from the base.

PROBLEMS

None.

* ✳ **PRETTY DAISY FLOWERS**
* ✳ **EVERGREEN GREYISH FOLIAGE**
* ✳ **SUITABLE FOR MOST SOILS**

SOLANUM

Solanum crispum

SITE AND SOIL A warm, sunny and sheltered position. Although best in deeper soils, tolerant of thin, alkaline conditions, too. Fairly hardy, tolerates -10°C (14°F) in winter.
SIZE 2m (6ft) after two years, up to 6m (20ft) eventually.
PROPAGATION Fairly easy, by cuttings.

❝ For once, we have here a strikingly distinctive twining climber, a touch on the tender side but not seriously so, that really is widely grown and appreciated. It is the only properly hardy climbing member of the potato family, a relationship betrayed immediately by the shape of its characteristic bluish summer flowers with purple anthers. And like most other members of the family, it originates in South America. In most areas it is more or less evergreen, but is durable enough to survive even after rather cold winters. Solanum crispum can be a trifle unkempt but a plant in full flower always arouses comment. ❞

CARE

Best grown over an extensive system of support wires against a tall, sheltered wall although it will be effective in a more open situation in milder areas. Although the best plants are usually on rich, deep soils, it has the singular attribute of being at its best in alkaline situations where admittedly, the soils are often

Solanum crispum 'Glasnevin'

RECOMMENDED VARIETIES
'Glasnevin' (sometimes called 'Autumnale') produces more flowers of a rich blue over a longer period in mild areas, well into the winter.

rather shallow. Mulch in late autumn and again in spring, preferably with garden compost or leaf mould. Give a balanced rose or other potash-rich fertilizer in spring.

PROPAGATION
Take softwood cuttings in early summer and strike them in a 50:50 mixture of sand and peat with bottom heat of about 25°C (77°F). Seed is often available but plants raised in this way are very variable and I don't recommend it.

PRUNING
Any pruning should be done with care, as some people develop allergic rashes to the foliage. Thin out in

Solanum jasminoides 'Album'

SIMILAR SPECIES
Solanum jasminoides (Potato Vine) is similar but with pale blue flowers and is less hardy. The true species is scarcely worth choosing but there is a lovely white flowered form, 'Album', that is a wonderful plant for a mild garden.

spring, removing overcrowded and browned shoots, but wait until the extent of winter cold damage can be seen. Where space is more limited, and especially in mild areas where growth may be vigorous, it can be cut back hard and will regenerate from old wood.

PROBLEMS
Aphids, whiteflies and viruses may be troublesome.

✳ **UNUSUAL, POTATO-LIKE FLOWERS**
✳ **VIGOROUS**
✳ **TOLERANT OF CHALKY SOILS**

Trachelospermum jasminoides Star Jasmine

SITE AND SOIL A warm, sheltered situation; preferably with a good loamy soil although tolerant of some soil dryness. Fairly hardy, tolerates -5 to -10°C (23-14°F) in winter.
SIZE 2m (6ft) after three years, up to 6-7m (20-23ft) eventually.
PROPAGATION Fairly easy, by layering.

> " *A gardening friend whom I see several times each year always prefaces our conversations with something along the lines of 'thank goodness you introduced me to* Trachelospermum'. *Seeing the way this wonderful oriental twining evergreen climber has established itself against an old brick wall in his fairly mild and sheltered garden, I can understand the sentiment. It is my regret that it has failed in mine, for the thick, glossy dark green leaves and white, remarkably jasmine-like flowers and fragrance make for a truly lovely plant. My garden is simply not warm enough, but I commend the plant with real feeling and admiration to anyone whose garden is.* "

Trachelospermum jasminoides

CARE
Although no doubt a tree-climber in its native environment, it is always seen to best advantage in a domestic situation when allowed to cling to a framework of wires tightly fixed against a warm wall. It is tolerant of moderately dry conditions, but is immeasurably better in a free-draining but moist, rather organic soil and will tolerate moderate alkalinity. Mulch in late autumn and again in spring, preferably with garden compost or leaf mould. Give a balanced rose or other potash-rich fertilizer in spring.

PROPAGATION
Like other members of the family Apocynaceae with milky sap, it can be difficult to strike from cuttings and the best method is by layering in autumn.

PRUNING
Prune in spring to remove any shoots damaged by winter cold and cut back long, straggly side-shoots to within about 15cm (6in) of a permanent framework of older stems in order to encourage flowering.

PROBLEMS
None.

RECOMMENDED VARIETIES
I find the true species much the most attractive flowering form. 'Variegatum' is less vigorous and has smaller leaves with whitish splash marks but looks a messy plant. 'Wilson 776' or 'Wilsonii' is a non-flowering form with green-bronze leaves.

SIMILAR SPECIES
Trachelospermum asiaticum, from Japan and Korea, is a similar though slightly less vigorous species with more yellowish flowers.

✳ **EXQUISITE PERFUME**
✳ **LUSH, GLOSSY EVERGREEN LEAVES**
✳ **DELIGHTFUL, JASMINE-LIKE FLOWERS**

VITIS

I realize that the name vine can have a fairly general meaning and is applied to a wide range of different types of climbing plant, but it has come to be associated especially with the grapevine, *Vitis vinifera*, and its close relatives. Although there is a long history of grape growing in Britain, commercial wine production went into serious decline until its revival over the past 20 years or so. And even though yields may be unpredictable in areas with climates like that of Britain, it does serve to demonstrate that grape growing outdoors is not as unrealistic a proposition as some would believe. I shan't enter here, however, into detailed methods of grape production for wine making but concentrate on the growing of vines outdoors principally for ornamental purposes, with a crop of grapes as a bonus.

Vitis vinifera Grapevine

❝ I rather doubt if there is a literature on any plant greater than that on the grapevine. It has, indeed, been an important cultivated crop for so long that its natural origin is now obscure, although it probably comes from the area extending from south-east Europe to south-western Asia. Its principle features are large deciduous leaves, grasping tendrils, tiny greenish flowers and, of course, the fruit, varying in both size and shape, and in colour from very pale green to almost black. There are numerous varieties, bred and selected for wine production in different areas but in marginal climates, such as that of Britain, rather few will succeed outdoors. And from a purely ornamental standpoint, the foliage with its attractive, if brief, autumn colours is really more important than the fruit. ❞

Vitis 'Brant'

SITE AND SOIL A warm, sheltered situation; tolerant of most soils but best with a good, slightly alkaline loam. Hardy, tolerates -15 to -20°C (5 to -4°F) in winter.
SIZE 2m (6ft) after three years, up to 8-9m (25-30ft) eventually, although usually confined by annual pruning.
PROPAGATION Easy, by cuttings.

CARE

Although vineyard grapes are grown in the open, trained against sets of horizontal wires, it makes more sense in a garden where only one or two are grown, to plant them like other climbers, tied to securely fixed horizontal wires on walls, stout trellises or similar structures. They soon become unmanageable if grown against a tree or similar support, although some gardeners manage to keep them under control and also produce a few grapes by allowing them fairly free rein over pergolas. Vines are tolerant of considerable alkalinity (some of the finest wines come from limestone sites) and of moderately dry conditions, but fruit production will be better from a free-draining but well manured soil. Mulch in late autumn and again in spring, preferably with well rotted manure; moisture is essential for fruit swelling. Give a balanced general or potash-rich fertilizer in spring.

PROPAGATION

Strikes readily from cuttings of which the best type are 'vine eyes' – short cuttings taken in late winter and bearing a single bud with about 1cm (½in) of stem either side of it. Push the cuttings into a 3:1 sand and soil-based potting compost mixture, such that the bud just protrudes above the surface, and place them in a covered propagator with bottom heat of about 25°C (77°F). It is pointless growing grapevines from seed as the fruiting varieties do not come true.

PRUNING

It is important to establish a permanent framework of stems or rods, so in the first season after planting, tie-in all of the vertical shoots fairly loosely to the wires. In the following winter, select the strongest two, three or rarely even more of these shoots (depending on the size of wall to be covered), cut them back by about half, and space them so they are positioned vertically but equidistantly, about 45cm (18in) apart, along the horizontal support wires. These will become the main rods and, each subsequent winter, the previous season's extension growth on them should be cut back by about half until they are as tall as space permits. Thereafter, all extension growth should be cut back each winter to just above the base.

Also each winter, cut back the side-shoots on the rods to two buds

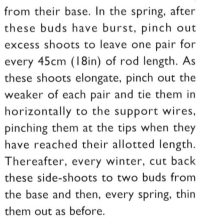

Vitis vinifera 'Purpurea'

RECOMMENDED VARIETIES (excluding greenhouse varieties)

Most of the wine grapes require a really warm sunny position. The following small selection is of varieties that I know will succeed in slightly cooler positions and make attractive ornamental subjects. 'Brant' (small black fruit, more of an ornamental than real fruiting variety and the only one that can be allowed relatively free rein without rigorous pruning), 'Chardonnay' (white), 'Müller-Thurgau' (white), 'Pinot Blanc' (white), 'Purpurea' (black with very attractive deep purple foliage), 'Schiava Grossa' (black).

from their base. In the spring, after these buds have burst, pinch out excess shoots to leave one pair for every 45cm (18in) of rod length. As these shoots elongate, pinch out the weaker of each pair and tie them in horizontally to the support wires, pinching them at the tips when they have reached their allotted length. Thereafter, every winter, cut back these side-shoots to two buds from the base and then, every spring, thin them out as before.

To encourage fruit production, and provided the vine is small enough to be manageable, it is worth giving some extra attention to the pruning. So, as the side-shoots elongate, look out for flowers arising on them and pinch out the shoot to a point just above two leaves beyond the flowers. In turn, further side-shoots (sub-laterals) may arise from the main side-shoots, and these should be

Vitis coignetiae

SIMILAR SPECIES

Vitis coignetiae is a vigorous vine with very large and beautiful leaves with fine autumn colours but barely edible fruit. It does not cling as efficiently as the grapevine and may need tying-in to its support. It is really at its best when allowed to grow over a large pergola or similar support.

pinched out just beyond the first leaf. Unlike greenhouse grape production, however, it really isn't worth going to the trouble of thinning out the fruit within the bunches on outdoor vines.

PROBLEMS

Mildew, red spider mite, grey mould (on fruit, see p. 22), scale insects.

✳ **VIGOROUS HABIT**

✳ **EDIBLE FRUIT**

✳ **ATTRACTIVE FOLIAGE WITH GOOD AUTUMN COLOURS**

WISTERIA

" Many gardeners have argued that the wisteria is the finest of all climbing plants; someone once called it the Queen of Climbers and most gardening writers since have followed suit. I shan't argue against its cause and would be a much sadder person without the plant that clothes the front wall of my own house. A wisteria, even a relatively young one, has an aged and gnarled appearance rivalled by little else and, in flower, it is quite simply unmatched by anything that can grow in a cold climate. The species planted most commonly are oriental: Wisteria sinensis, *from China, which twines anti-clockwise, and* W. floribunda, *from Japan, which twines clockwise. It takes only a cursory glance at their flowers (which in most forms are attractively fragrant) to realize they belong to the pea family and the only real frustration comes from the fact that these flowers can be rather a long time in coming; it's usually five years before any wisteria blooms and seven before it does so prolifically. Wisterias climb by means of twining stems and, left untended, will very soon become an untidy knotted mass of botanical rope; they are worthy of a little of your care, therefore, and will reward you for it admirably. "*

SITE AND SOIL Tolerant of most soils and most aspects although best in sun. Hardy, tolerates -15 to -20°C (5 to -4°F) in winter although late hard frost can sometimes damage the blossoms.
SIZE 2m (6ft) after two years, up to 9-15m (30-50ft) eventually if unpruned.
PROPAGATION Fairly easy, by layering.

Wisteria floribunda **'Multijuga'**

Wisteria sinensis

CARE

Although wisterias undoubtedly flower best in full sun on a warm wall, my own plant grows on a cool, fairly shady wall yet still gives a fine display, so they are worth planting in almost any aspect. In the early stages, they are best tied in to very firmly fixed horizontal support wires but as the plant ages, these become inadequate and the best system then is to use strategically positioned vine eyes, screwed to secure wall plugs, and tie the individual stems to these with strong plastic-coated tying wire. But do check and re-tie the stems each year, for the annual growth in girth is considerable and the tie that was loose one year can strangle the stems by the next. Despite their great size and vigour, wisterias have a low water demand and thus pose

Wisteria venusta

Wisteria floribunda 'Alba'

RECOMMENDED VARIETIES

Varieties of *Wisteria floribunda*: 'Alba' (white), 'Multijuga', also called 'Macrobotrys' (violet-purple, huge racemes up to 60cm (24in) long), 'Rosea' (rose-pink), 'Snow Showers' (white), 'Violacea Plena' (violet-purple, double flowers). Varieties of *Wisteria sinensis*: the true species with lilac flowers is commonly planted; also 'Alba' (white), 'Prolific' (lilac-blue).

Wisteria x formosa

no threat to wall foundations, even on relatively heavy clays. They are tolerant of all soils but will not succeed on very shallow sites. In the early stages, mulch in late autumn and again in spring and give rose or other potash-rich fertilizer in spring. Old and well established plants require little such attention.

PROPAGATION

Layering in late autumn is the most reliable method. In some years, long, seed-containing pods may be produced, but the best varieties do not come true and it is a waste of time raising plants from seed. Commercial plants should always be grafted.

PRUNING

In the first season after planting, tie-in all of the vertical shoots fairly loosely to the support wires. In the following winter, select between three and five shoots (depending on the space available) to form the main framework of the plant, cut them back by half, spread them so they are spaced more or less equidistantly, and tie them to the support wires.

Thereafter, in late summer each year, cut back all of the long whippy side-shoots to about 25cm (10in) in length, except for any that you may need to fill in gaps in the main framework. In the following winter, cut these shortened shoots back further to three buds from the base.

PROBLEMS

None.

✳ **SUPERB EYE-CATCHING FLOWERS**

✳ **VERY EASY TO GROW**

✳ **ATTRACTIVE AUTUMN FOLIAGE COLOUR**

Caiophora lateritia

SITE AND SOIL A warm, sunny position, tolerant of most free-draining soils. Barely hardy, tolerates -5°C (23°F).
SIZE 3m (10ft).

66 *This is an unexpectedly lovely South American oddity, a member of a fairly large plant family, the Loascaceae, that has almost no other garden representatives. But no matter, for* Caiophora *is a fine, if slightly antisocial, twining climber bearing stinging bristles (although they are generally ineffective on young plants at transplanting size). But forget, if you can, the foliage and grow it for its long-stalked five-petalled flowers that, in the wild, are usually red but in the cultivated forms pass through white, apricot and reddish shades and look more like single roses than anything else that springs to mind. In due course, curious and tightly spiralled seed pods form and are, in their way, almost more appealing. Yes, this really is a head turning species.* 99

Caiphora lateritia

RECOMMENDED VARIETIES
The true species is sometimes available but you are more likely to see a selection called 'Frothy'.

CARE
Raise by the half-hardy annual technique and plant out after the danger of the last frost has passed. It is always at its best when grown in an informal situation; allowed to scramble over and through mediterranean style shrubs and perennials in a warm, dry and sunny spot. In mild areas, it is best grown as a tender perennial with the top growth cut back and a protective mulch applied around the crown in autumn. I have seen *Caiophora* grown very successfully as a conservatory plant in pots of a soil-based compost although even then, it must be said that it is a fairly short-lived species and if you have space, it might be easiest to grow it on a biennial basis, raising seedlings regularly each year for flowering in the next.

PROBLEMS
None.
* **STRIKINGLY UNUSUAL FLOWERS AND SEED PODS**
* **VIGOROUS**
* **EASY TO GROW**

Cobaea scandens Cup and Saucer Vine, Cathedral Bells

SITE AND SOIL A warm, sunny position, tolerant of most free-draining soils. Tender.
SIZE 4m (13ft).

Cobaea scandens

66 *One of the best known of climbers raised from seed, this is an astonishingly vigorous Mexican plant that will easily cover a reasonably sized pergola in a season with the aid of its twining stems and tendrils. The cup-shaped and slightly sinister appearing long-stalked flowers are unusually coloured; more or less green at first but becoming increasingly purplish as they age. Sometimes, there is a pronounced, heavy perfume but this doesn't seem to be invariable. The only real disappointment, as with other vigorous annuals, is that it all comes to an end in the autumn although* Cobaea *can be grown as a perennial in a conservatory.* 99

CARE

Raise by the half-hardy annual technique, sowing the seeds on their sides after soaking them overnight in slightly tepid water and plant out after the danger of the last frost has passed. The variegated form does not come true from seed and should, therefore, be bought as a plant and propagated by cuttings. To do this, cut back an outdoor plant to about

RECOMMENDED VARIETIES
'Alba' is a striking white flowered form and 'Variegata' one with variegated foliage, although both are scarce.

30cm (12in) in autumn, pot it up and take it into the protection of a greenhouse to overwinter. Strike shoot-tip cuttings in spring in a 3:1 sand and soil-based compost mixture in a propagator with bottom heat of 22-25°C (72-77°F). *Cobaea* is better than most annual climbers in the more formal setting of a tall wall but still probably best when allowed to grow over some old outbuilding or large shrub. Will grow satisfactorily in most soils provided they are not too wet or too rich, the latter condition markedly depressing flowering.

PROBLEMS
Red spider mites, whiteflies, aphids.

✳ **HANDSOME, UNUSUALLY COLOURED FLOWERS**

✳ **VIGOROUS**

✳ **EASY TO GROW**

Cobaea scandens

CODONOPSIS Climbing Bellflowers

SITE AND SOIL Most aspects, but best in sun and preferably with a good, moisture-retentive loam. Moderately hardy, tolerates -15°C (5°F).
SIZE 2m (6ft).

“ *The very idea of climbing bellflowers is appealing and* Codonopsis, *a relative of* Campanula, *is precisely that. There are several species, all from Asia, some alpine that are pretty tough. Most have tuberous roots and some are usually bought and grown as herbaceous perennials although the commonest,* Codonopsis convolvulacea *is most likely to be encountered as an annual. It is a genuine and enthusiastic twiner, both the stems and the stalks that bear the bluish-violet rather vinca-like flowers twisting around any convenient support. I'm delighted to see that several nursery catalogues now list a number of other species and this is an entire genus of climbing plants that could, with real justification, be grown and seen much more widely than it is now.* ”

Codonopsis convolvulacea

CARE

Although hardy, it is best raised by the half-hardy annual technique. Pinch out the shoot tips at least once in the early stages to produce a dense cover. Once established, it can be treated as a normal herbaceous perennial, cutting back above-ground growth to 30cm (12in) above soil level in autumn, mulching with compost and then cutting back to soil level in spring once new shoots emerge. Established plants may be propagated by division in spring. Plant in any aspect, although flowering will be best in full sun and with slightly moist, acidic soil. Although *Codonopsis* can be grown against a wall, the cover will be lost when it is cut back in autumn, and it is better when allowed to scramble through and over small shrubs such as heathers.

PROBLEMS

None.

✱ **Pretty, bell-like flowers**
✱ **Vigorous**
✱ **Hardy and easy to grow**

SIMILAR SPECIES

Codonopsis lanceolata, from China, has purplish stems that reach about 1m (3ft) with lovely flowers, characteristically bell-shaped but very pale blue with purple spots and lines.
Codonopsis tangshen, from China, is more vigorous, reaching about 3m (10ft) with more unusual flowers – yellowish-green with deep purple spotting. It is probably the hardiest of the common climbing species, tolerating -15 to -20°C (5 to -4°F).

SITE AND SOIL Full sun with deep, manure-rich soil. Tender.
SIZE Up to 9m (30ft).

❝ I always think it a shame that the numerous vegetable gardeners who grow marrows and cucumbers don't appreciate the ornamental value of their very close relatives, the gourds, which can be grown either as trailers or climbers. They belong to several different genera: many are in Cucurbita, *but the bottle gourds are derived from* Lagenaria siceraria, *and the vegetable sponge from* Luffa cylindrica. *They originate from tropical and sub-tropical parts of the world and are, therefore, distinctly tender. They, nonetheless, grow very rapidly during the course of the summer to produce most attractive, usually golden flowers and then the familiar, swollen fruits in an astonishing array of size, shape and colour. Even at the end of the growing season, their appeal is not lost for they may be harvested, dried and used as ornaments. ❞*

CARE

Raise by the half-hardy annual technique, sowing the flat seeds on their sides and plant out after the danger of the last frost has passed. Plant against some robust, informal support which can hold up both the rather fragile, brittle stems as well as the considerable weight of the fruits. Gourds must have a moist, very rich soil and a sunny, warm position and should be mulched, watered regularly

Gourd 'Karrella Gourd'

Ornamental gourds

and fed weekly with a balanced high-potash liquid feed.

PROBLEMS

Mildew, viruses, aphids, root and stem rots.
* ✳ **VIGOROUS SCRAMBLING HABIT**
* ✳ **FASCINATING FRUITS**
* ✳ **EASY TO GROW**

Gourd 'Turk's turban'

Cucurbita ficifolia **(Malabar Gourd)**

ECCREMOCARPUS

Eccremocarpus scaber Glory Vine

SITE AND SOIL Most aspects, but best in sun and preferably with a good, moisture-retentive loam. Barely hardy, tolerates -5°C (23°F). **SIZE** 2-3m (6-10ft).

> *Eccremocarpus, from Chile, is perhaps the classic example of a climber that is most familiar to gardeners as an annual to be raised from seed, but that surprises many in the fact that it is a true perennial and will survive outdoors for a few years, at least in mild areas. Eventually it does begin to deteriorate and is never very long lived. But either as an annual or a perennial, it has some splendid attributes: attractive, finely divided leaves with tendrils, a mass of nodding, reddish-orange tubular flowers with an almost wax-like appearance, a very long flowering season from early summer until well into the autumn and, even at the end of that, appealingly inflated seed pods. Yes, it is a very good plant indeed and glory vine is a very apt name.* 💬

CARE

Raise by the half-hardy annual technique. Sow early in the spring in order to obtain large, well grown plants for putting out. Pinch out the shoot tips at least once in the early stages to produce a denser cover. It can be grown on trellis against a wall but is better over shrubs, evergreen hedges or even used to cover wire fences. It will always flower best in full sun and in a fairly rich, moisture-

Eccremocarpus scaber

retentive soil with no tendency to waterlogging. Give liquid feed high in potash every two weeks during the summer. In mild areas, cut back above-ground growth to the woody rootstock, cutting off most in autumn but leaving about 30cm (12in) as protection until the spring. Apply a mulch of compost to afford extra protection in winter. In the very mildest areas, the top growth too

Eccremocarpus scaber

may survive, and should simply be cut back by between a quarter and a third in the spring. But, in any event, plants are best renewed every four or five years.

PROBLEMS

None.

✳ **MASSES OF VIVIDLY COLOURED FLOWERS**

✳ **VIGOROUS**

✳ **VERY EASY TO GROW**

SITE AND SOIL Full sun in fairly good soil. Tender.
SIZE 3-5m (10-16ft).

❝ Never was it more true that one man's weed is another's prized garden plant. Yes, throughout the tropics, species of Ipomoea, _the morning glories, take the place of their close temperate climate relatives, the bindweeds. They will be found scrambling through hedgerows and above the high tide mark on beaches. There is even one important crop plant, the sweet potato, in the genus. But they also make excellent half-hardy garden climbers with their large, funnel-shaped and typically blue or mauve coloured flowers and rapid twining growth. They are especially useful and effective when growing up wire fences or netting although, of course, unlike the real bindweeds, they and their screening effect vanish with the first autumn frosts. Also unlike the bindweeds, they will never become out of hand, invasive or persistent in the soil. ❞_

Ipomoea purpurea

RECOMMENDED VARIETIES

There are three common species of _Ipomoea_ that have been used to raise garden ornamentals. _Ipomoea purpurea_ is usually seen as the true species, with its variable flowers of purple, blue, reddish and white in various combinations. All can be expected from a seed lot, although selections are sometimes called 'Alba', 'Rosea' and so forth.
I. nil has given rise to most of the cultivated varieties such as 'Early Call' (usually red with white tube), 'Cardinal' (red), 'Flying Saucers' (blue and white), 'Scarlett O'Hara' (scarlet) and 'Heavenly Blue' (sky-blue). _I. hederacea_ has yielded 'Roman Candy' (cerise with white edge and tube, leaves mottled with white – hard to imagine if you have never seen it).

Ipomoea 'Cardinal'

SIMILAR SPECIES

Ipomoea lobata, from Mexico, has very distinctive and different flowers – red, fading to orange, tubular with markedly protruding stamens, and grouped in a one-sided raceme. It is very vigorous, reaching 5-7m (16-23ft) in two years, but really achieves little of its potential in the first season. Being barely hardy, it is best treated as a biennial, grown in a container and taken into shelter overwinter.

CARE

Raise by the half-hardy annual technique after soaking the seeds for about 12 hours in slightly tepid water. Sow the seeds in pairs into small pots and pull out the weaker if both germinate. Harden-off very thoroughly and plant out after the danger of the last frost has passed, but transplant with care for they resent root disturbance. Pinch out the shoot tips at least once in the early stages to produce a denser cover. Best grown against a support, such as small meshed trellis or wire, that offers plenty of scope for twining through. Must have full sun for good flowering and a fairly rich and well drained soil. In the tropics, you will certainly see them growing in impoverished soils but this only seems successful where temperatures are very high.

PROBLEMS

None.

✳ **BRILLIANTLY COLOURED FLOWERS**
✳ **VIGOROUS**
✳ **VERY EASY TO GROW**

LATHYRUS Sweet Pea

SITE AND SOIL Full sun in good, moisture-retentive soil. Fairly hardy, tolerates -5 to -10°C (23-14°F) as young plants.
SIZE 2-3m (6-10ft) (with some dwarfs).

“ *As the gardening years go by, I am more than ever convinced that there is no finer summer-flowering annual, be it climber or not, than the sweet pea. And there is surely no finer flower of any type for cutting. The combination of a quite deliciously fresh and light fragrance, a range of generally soft pastel colours, dainty flowers, long stems and a multitude of blooms over a long period is quite simply unrivalled. Yet sweet peas are not exactly simple to grow, at least not to grow well. They require fairly continuous attention if they are to give of their best and they are rather demanding in their site requirements. But conversely, they have a helpful versatility and may be trained in a number of very attractive ways. The modern garden sweet pea is derived from the mediterranean* Lathyrus odoratus, *but it is a species that has been a part of gardening for centuries and seems long ago to have lost its southern tenderness. Developed from it also, and embraced by the name sweet pea, are now a number of rather distinct types. There are also a couple of closely related perennial species,* L. grandiflorus *and* L. latifolius, *and I have included them here for convenience.* ”

Lathyrus grandiflorus

CARE

Sweet peas should be raised by the hardy annual technique but there are a number of different ways of doing this (see right). The seeds of different varieties vary considerably in colour (ranging from almost black to almost white), size and surface texture – some are smooth and some markedly wrinkled. In all cases, however, the seeds should be soaked overnight in very slightly tepid water. Those that float should be rejected as non-viable while those that sink but fail to swell (as happens particularly with dark seeded varieties) should be nicked with the point of a very sharp knife on the side of the seed away from the 'eye' and then soaked for a few more hours.

There are four main ways and

There are several main groups of garden interest:

So-called old-fashioned or Grandiflora varieties, with rather few, small and plain edged but intensely fragrant flowers: 'Dorothy Eckford' (white), 'Lord Nelson' (dark blue), 'Queen Alexandra' (crimson).

'Normal' garden or Spencer varieties, with up to five larger wavy-edged flowers per stem: 'Champagne Bubbles' (cream-pink), 'Midnight' (dark maroon), 'Queen Mother' (salmon-pink), 'Royal Wedding' (white), 'Sheila Macqueen' (salmon-orange).

Galaxy varieties, with up to eight flowers per stem: usually found as 'Galaxy Mixed'.

Mammoth varieties, with up to seven flowers per stem: usually found as 'Mammoth Mixed'.

Dwarf varieties, which reach barely 30cm (12in) in height and may be grown in containers with minimal support: 'Bijou' (mixture), 'Cupid' (mixture), 'Patio' (mixture), 'Snoopea' (mixture).

Intermediate or Semi-Dwarf varieties which reach about 1m (3ft): 'Continental', 'Jet-Set', and 'Knee-High' (all mixtures).

And finally, in a class of its own, 'Matucana', deep purple and blue, intensely frangrant and very old.

times of sowing: in pots in the autumn for overwintering in a cold frame and planting out in the spring; directly in the flowering positions in the autumn; in pots in late winter for

Lathyrus odoratus

Lathyrus 'Snoopea'

hardening-off and planting out in spring; or directly in the flowering positions in spring. After considerable trial and error, I prefer the third option which seems to give strong plants and quick establishment with the least check to growth.

Sweet peas produce better plants if grown in pots slightly deeper than usual to accommodate the long tap root and it is possible to buy special sweet pea pots – tall in relation to their diameter. There is some merit in making your own tall pots from rolls of paper as these can then be planted out entire, with no disturbance to the root system. The seeds should be sown, two to a pot and the weaker removed if both germinate. As soon as the plants have two true leaves the tips should be pinched out to encourage bushiness.

Lathyrus 'Royal Wedding'

SITE AND SOIL

A sunny position is essential; in more than very light shade, sweet peas will be miserable plants. The soil must be moisture-retentive yet with no tendency to waterlogging and, ideally, is a rich medium loam in which plenty of manure or compost have been incorporated to a depth of about 45cm (18in). You may read of deep and thorough trenching being done for sweet peas but this is only necessary with plants that are grown for exhibition purposes. To produce flowers for normal garden display and cutting for the home, much less labour is needed.

Lathyrus grandiflorus

SUPPORT

To grow sweet peas with huge flowers and very long stems, the plants must be grown by the cordon system, which entails the careful training of one or two leading stems and the removal of side-shoots, much as is done with tomatoes. I am confident, however, that for garden purposes, perfectly acceptable and beautiful flowers will be produced with no side-shooting and the minimum of tying. The main methods of support are against clematis netting or trellis on a wall, through tall shrubs, up a more or less cylindrical arrangement of netting or canes, or up a wigwam of tall twiggy sticks or canes. My own preference is for the latter which not only gives very good results but also looks most attractive *in situ*. Growing the plants against walls is seldom a very satisfactory method, for it is almost impossible to maintain the soil in a sufficiently moist condition.

The ideal diameter for a wigwam support is about 1m (3ft) with approximately 15cm (6in) between plants (giving a total of about 20 plants around the circumference). If canes rather than twigs are used, it will almost certainly be necessary to tie the stems loosely to them initially, to encourage climbing and it will also be found beneficial to tie some strings around the wigwam to give additional supports for the tendrils.

Mulch after planting with well rotted compost, water regularly during the summer and give a liquid fertilizer high in potash once a week. The flowers must be picked regularly; once some begin to set seed, flower production will decline markedly.

PROBLEMS

Aphids, mildew, slugs and snails (on young plants), red spider mites, thrips, root and stem basal rots. The last of these will be serious if the soil is cold and wet, and can build up over a period of years of repeated cropping. But because there is often only one really suitable spot for sweet peas in a small garden, my advice is to continue to grow them in the same place until dark stem lesions, root rotting and poor growth indicate a build up of fungus in the soil. In recent seasons, pollen beetles have become a serious nuisance on sweet peas, coincident with the increase in growing the oil seed rape crops on which they proliferate. The small black beetles enter the flowers, become trapped within and, especially on paler coloured types, are visible from the outside. Unfortunately, no-one has yet produced a satisfactory remedy.

❋ **SUPERB PERFUME**
❋ **DELIGHTFUL FOR CUTTING**
❋ **HUGE RANGE OF COLOURS**

Lathyrus latifolius

MAURANDELLA

Maurandella antirrhinifolia Climbing Snapdragon

SITE AND SOIL A warm, sunny wall, preferably with a good, moderately rich, moisture-retentive loam. Tender.
SIZE 2m (6ft).

    ❝ *For once, a plant with a similar common name and a similar appearance to a familiar garden species is related to it; the old genus name* Asarina *is, in fact, the Spanish name for the snapdragon and both are near relatives in the family Scrophulariaceae. But unlike the real* Antirrhinum, Maurandella, *from California and adjoining parts of the United States, has been almost unknown in european gardens until recently. This is a great pity, for it isn't as if there are legions of annual climbers. In practice, M. antirrhinifolia is generally best grown as an annual, although it can also be treated as a tender perennial. The wild species has deep violet flowers but red coloured variants also occur, with the small flowers borne along the twining stems. They are vigorous plants, too aggressive for hanging baskets, but lovely scrambling through old shrubs, up and over fences, netting and similar supports.* ❞

Maurandella antirrhinifolia

CARE

Raise by the half-hardy annual technique. Germination can be slow but once the seedlings have emerged, growth is rapid and the shoot tips should be pinched out at least once in the early stages to produce a dense cover. Alternatively, and especially if you obtain a particularly good colour strain, take tip cuttings in late summer and strike them in a 50:50 mixture of sand and soil-based potting compost in a propagator with bottom heat of about 25°C (77°F). Overwinter the young plants under frost-free cover and plant them out after the last frosts in spring. Plant in a warm, sunny position with fairly rich, moisture-retentive soil.

PROBLEMS

None.

✻ **DAINTY, SNAPDRAGON-LIKE FLOWERS**
✻ **VIGOROUS**
✻ **EASY TO GROW**

Maurandya barclayana

SIMILAR SPECIES

Maurandya barclayana, from Mexico, one of several unrelated types of plant called Angel's Trumpets, is more vigorous, reaching about 3m (10ft), and has rather striking pink, purple or white flowers.

Maurandya scandens, also from Mexico, will reach about 3m (10ft) and occurs naturally in pink and violet shades, but pure purple strains and a selected mixture called 'Jewel Mixed' that includes white are also available.

RECOMMENDED VARIETIES

The only variety I have seen for raising from seed is a mixture (imaginatively called 'Mixed') of red and purple flowered plants, from which selections could be made.

Maurandya scandens

Maurandya scandens

RHODOCHITON

Rhodochiton atrosanguineus

SITE AND SOIL Full sun to light shade in free-draining soil. Tender.
SIZE 2m (6ft) within one season from seed; 3m (10ft) from established plants.

❝ *This most intriguing twining climber from Mexico has unofficially been called the parachute plant and, having looked at its flowers and used a trifle of imagination, you will appreciate why. They do indeed have something of the shape of a dark purple parachute, although with an abnormally large and even darker parachutist suspended beneath. Although it is tender, I wish it was grown more frequently as an outdoor annual than in its usual role as a greenhouse perennial where it seldom gives of its best, for it is so irresistible to whiteflies.* ❞

CARE

Raise by the half-hardy annual technique, preferably using fresh seed. If older packeted seed must be used, germination will be slow and erratic. An alternative approach is to obtain a stock plant, cut this back each autumn, pot it up for storage in a frost-free greenhouse, and then strike softwood cuttings in a 3:1 mixture of sand and soil-based compost in spring with bottom heat of 25°C (77°F). It requires light, fairly rich soil in a warm sunny position with shelter from winds. Ideally trained onto trellis against a warm wall but can also be grown in a container of soil-based potting compost (it is not as successful in soilless mixtures) and trained up a wigwam of canes or other supports. Feed weekly with potash-rich liquid fertilizer.

Rhodochiton atrosanguineus

PROBLEMS

Whiteflies, aphids.

✳ **STRIKINGLY UNUSUAL FLOWERS**
✳ **MODERATELY VIGOROUS**
✳ **EASY TO GROW**

Thunbergia alata
Black-Eyed Susan

SITE AND SOIL Full sun to light shade in free-draining soil. Tender.
SIZE 1m (3ft).

" Gardeners can become very possessive about their favourite plants, and ever since I discovered this very pretty little twining African climber some years ago, I have been protective towards it almost to the extent of wishing that no-one else grew it. But they do, and it is now to be found in most seed catalogues if not yet in most gardens. In the best forms, the flowers are rich yellow but there are now paler yellow and white variants too. Unlike most annual climbers, it isn't too vigorous and is perfectly at home in hanging baskets where, unlike almost everything else, it has the singular merit of going upwards to embrace the chains. And in case anyone is confused, no, it isn't the only plant known as Black-eyed Susan. "

CARE
Raise by the half-hardy annual technique; germination is easy and excellent. But like *Rhodochiton*, it can also be grown as a perennial by overwintering a stock plant and taking cuttings in spring, something that would be worthwhile if you found a particularly good colour strain. Unlike *Rhodochiton* it will flower perfectly well in its first year from seed. Due to its low vigour, it is ideally grown in a hanging basket or other container where it will be most successful in a soil-based compost. It is also very effective in a free-standing pot, trained up a small cane wigwam. Fairly tolerant of dryness but should be fed every two weeks with high-potash liquid fertilizer during the summer.

PROBLEMS
None.

* **PRETTY SINGLE FLOWERS**
* **NOT VIGOROUS**
* **VERY EASY TO GROW**

RECOMMENDED VARIETIES
I am convinced that the best strains of the true species give flowers of much the most attractive orange colour. But you are now more likely to see rather insipid mixtures such as 'Susie' with flowers of yellow, orange and white, some even lacking the attractive black central eye.

SIMILAR SPECIES
Thunbergia erecta (Clock Vine) is more vigorous, growing up to 2m (6ft), with larger flowers of cream-white and deep purple (or white in the variety 'Alba'). It is really more effective as a tender greehouse perennial.
Thunbergia fragrans is a more woody plant with larger, white flowers, usually offered as 'Angel Wings'.

Thunbergia alata

Thunbergia erecta

TROPAEOLUM Nasturtium

" Tropaeolum *must be the single most useful genus of annual and herbaceous climbers, with four rather distinct species contributing to paint walls, fences and, more especially, hedges, old shrubs and waste areas with the most fresh and vivid oranges and yellows right through the summer. They all originate in Central and South America and are conveniently divided into two groups – on the one hand, the red or orange flowered climbing nasturtium* Tropaeolum majus *and the yellow canary creeper,* T. peregrinum, *the former a true annual, the latter a tender perennial grown as such; and on the other,* T. speciosum *the rich red Scots flame flower, and its close relative* T. tuberosum, *which are hardy enough to be grown as herbaceous perennials in most areas.* "

Tropaeolum 'Whirly Bird'

Annual species

CARE

Raise *Tropaeolum peregrinum* by the half-hardy annual technique in pots. Growth is rapid so do not sow too early in the season. Harden-off very thoroughly before planting out. It is best grown in light, fairly rich soil in a warm sunny position with shelter from winds. Although fairly vigorous, it can be grown to dramatic effect in hanging baskets if it is allowed to hang down from a fairly high position. Feed weekly with potash-rich liquid fertilizer. *T. majus* is best sown *in situ* shortly before the danger of the last frosts has passed. It requires a sunny position but will only flower well in poor soil; in good growing conditions, it will merely produce lush foliage and, for this reason, is not successful in containers or in the company of other plants that require fertilizer. The flowers make delightful additions to summer salads.

RECOMMENDED VARIETIES
Tropaeolum peregrinum is usually available only as the true species. *T. majus* occurs as non-climbing forms too; the climbing types are offered in mixtures of reds, yellows and true oranges with such names as 'Climbing Mixed'. There are also double-flowered and variegated varieties and, in 'Jewel of Africa', the first variegated climber.

Tropaeolum majus

PROBLEMS

Large white butterflies – the caterpillars seem to prefer *Tropaeolum* to cabbages.

Perennial species

CARE

Although seed may be seen for sale, both species are best bought as plants. *Tropaeolum speciosum* has a rhizome which should be planted in well prepared, humus-rich soil, preferably against a dark evergreen hedge over which the trailing shoots will scramble. *T. tuberosum* has large, pretty red and yellow tubers which should be planted in similarly prepared soil, about 10cm (4in) deep. Both should be mulched with compost or leaf mould in spring and again in autumn, although in colder areas, the less hardy *T. tuberosum* is better lifted and the tubers stored like dahlias over-winter. Feed with balanced general or rose fertilizer in spring.

PROBLEMS

Large white butterfly caterpillars will eat the foliage, but are less serious than on the annual species.

* **VIVID FLOWER COLOURS**
* **MODERATELY VIGOROUS**
* **VERY EASY TO GROW**

RECOMMENDED VARIETIES

Tropaeolum speciosum is available only as the true species but there are variants of *T. tuberosum*, most notably 'Ken Aslet' with orange rather than red flowers.

Tropaeolum speciosum

Tropaeolum tuberosum

Tropaeolum peregrinum

INDEX

Page numbers in italics refer to illustrations.

PHOTOGRAPHIC ACKNOWLEDGMENTS

A-Z Botanical Collection 78 /**K Jayakam** 68 Bottom Right
Professor Stefan Buczacki 34 Top
Eric Crichton 1 Bottom, 5 Right, 7, 12 Top, 13 Top, 13 Bottom,
22 Bottom, 24, 27 Bottom Right, 33 Bottom Left, 39 Top, 48
Bottom Right, 52 Centre Left, 53, 58 Top Right, 58 Bottom Left, 59,
61 left, 63 left, 63 Centre, 64, 66 Bottom Left, 66 Top Left, 70
Bottom, 75 Bottom, 77 Top, 77 Bottom Left, 82 left, 83 left, 84, 85
left, 93 Bottom Left
John Glover 5 left, 14, 34 Bottom Left, 40 Bottom, 43 left, 46 Top
Left, 46 Bottom Left, 47 Right, 48 Bottom Centre, 55, 57, 65, 66
Top Right, 75 Top, 76 left, 77 Bottom Right, 90, 93 Top Right
Derek Gould 46 Bottom Right, 54 Top, 73, 80
Andrew Lawson 4, 6 Bottom, 8, 12 Bottom, 18 left, 28 Top, 31
Bottom Right, 36 Top, 37 Top, 49, 51, 68 Bottom Left, 68 Top, 73
Right, 87
Photos Horticultural 2 Top, 6 Top, 11, 17, 19, 20, 22 Top, 23, 27
Bottom Left, 27 Top Right, 28 Bottom, 30 Top, 31 Top Left, 31

Bottom Left, 32, 38 left, 40 Top, 41, 42, 44, 46 Bottom Centre, 47
left, 52 Right, 54 Bottom, 56 Right, 61 Centre, 61 Right, 63 Right,
69, 70 Top, 71, 72 left, 81 Top Left, 81 Top Right, 85 Bottom, 85
Right, 86, 89 Bottom Left, 89 Top Left, 92 Bottom
Reed Consumer Books Ltd./Michael Boys 29 Bottom, 34
Centre, 52 Top Left, 60 /**Jerry Harpur** 33 Top Centre /**Andrew
Lawson** front cover background, front cover right inset,1 Top, 2-3
Background /**Steve Wooster** front cover left inset, back cover
/**George Wright** 25, 26, 35 Bottom, 67
Harry Smith Collection 15, 16, 18 Right, 21, 29 Top, 29 Centre,
30 Bottom, 35 Top, 36 Bottom, 37 Bottom, 38 Right, 39 Bottom, 43
Right, 45, 48 Bottom Left, 48 Top, 50, 56 left, 58 Top Left, 58
Bottom Right, 62 Top, 62 Bottom, 74, 76 Right, 79 Bottom, 79 Top,
81 Bottom Right, 81 Bottom Left, 82 Right, 89 Bottom Right, 91
Top, 92 Top, 93 Bottom Right
Suttons Seeds 83 Right, 91 Bottom
Derry Watkins 88

TEMPERATURE CHART

BARELY HARDY	0°C to -5°C	32°F to 23°F
FAIRLY HARDY	-5°C to -10°C	23°F to 14°F
MODERATELY HARDY	-10°C to -15°C	14°F to 5°F
HARDY	-15°C to -20°C	5°F to -4°F
VERY HARDY	-20°C or below	-4°F or below